THE
LIBERATING
LAW

THE LIBERATING LAW

10 STEPS TO FREEDOM

GERARD REED

Beacon Hill Press of Kansas City
Kansas City, Missouri

Copyright 1996
by Beacon Hill Press of Kansas City

ISBN 083-411-6170

Printed in the
United States of America

Cover Design: Paul Franitza

Library of Congress Cataloging-in-Publication Data

Reed, Gerard.
    Liberating law : ten steps to freedom / Gerard Reed.
        p.   cm.
    ISBN 0-8341-1617-0 (pbk.)
        1. Ten commandments—Criticism, interpretation, etc.
2. Christian ethics—Nazarene authors.   I. Title.
BV4655.R44   1996
222'.1606—dc20   95-51508
                                                        CIP

10 9 8 7 6 5 4 3 2 1

To Roberta, my wife,
whose optimism and goodness grace my life,

and to Don Hughes, longtime Nazarene Publishing
House representative, without whose prodding and
encouragement this book would not have been written.

CONTENTS

PART 1: A WORLD WANTING FREEDOM

1. Wanted: Some Imperatives!   11

2. The Covenant Context   23

PART 2: TEN STEPS TO FREEDOM

3. A Sacred Trust   49
   Old Testament Foundation: No Other Gods
   New Testament Internalization: Serve God

4. A Sacrosanct Focus   64
   Old Testament Foundation: No Idols Allowed
   New Testament Internalization: What's Really Living?

5. A Hallowed Name Above All Names   78
   Old Testament Foundation: Take Not God's Name in Vain
   New Testament Internalization: How to Hallow God's Name

6. A Sanctified Cosmos   93
   Old Testament Foundation: Living Sabbatically
   New Testament Internalization: A New Day for the New Way

7. The Sanctity of the Family   108
   Old Testament Foundation: Honor Your Father and Mother
   New Testament Internalization: Doing Our Father's Business

8. The Sanctity of Life   122
   Old Testament Foundation: Do Not Murder
   New Testament Internalization: Nurse No Anger

9. The Sanctity of Sex   137
   Old Testament Foundation: Adultery? No!
   New Testament Internalization: Chastity? Yes!

10. The Sanctity of Property   151
    Old Testament Foundation: Do Not Steal
    *New Testament Internalization: Living Honestly by Making
    an Honest Living*

11. The Sanctity of Our Word   164
    Old Testament Foundation: No False Witnesses
    New Testament Internalization: Truthful Tongues

12. The Sanctity of Satisfaction   178
    Old Testament Foundation: Do Not Covet
    *New Testament Internalization: Simplicity—When All You've Ever
    Wanted Isn't Enough*

Notes   195

Resources for Further Reading   203

I will walk at liberty,
For I seek Thy precepts.
—Ps. 119:45, NASB

PART ONE

A World
Wanting Freedom

1

Wanted: Some Imperatives!

"Let's face it," says Ann Landers. "America is sick."[1] The sickness whereof she speaks is a plague of immorality more devastating than the AIDS (*acquired immunodeficiency syndrome*) virus. From the urbane white-collar con artists who subverted the savings and loan industry to urban teenagers "wilding" and "tagging," something has subverted America's morality. Yet exactly what has happened, exactly why we're so troubled, is generally more confused than clarified by television panelists or newspaper pundits or congressional hearings.

An ancient explanation rooted in the Christian tradition argues that the land's sickness stems from failing to know the truth of our own moral nature. Embedded in human nature is an abiding reality, an ethical vein more precious than platinum. Doing right, we live according to its structure; doing wrong, we violate its essence. We humans share a common nature: living creatures designed in God's image and likeness, animated by our Creator, coded to live out His standards. So living rightly requires religious roots. Forsaking the vision of our divinely designed character, we forgo the capacity to do good. During this century, religion, as the source of morality, has been replaced with personal feelings and societal programs, giving us the bloodiest 100 years on record. Just as evil is "live" spelled backward, the loss of morality leads to the loss of life.

One of the keys to understanding what has happened in America resides in the values that emerged in the 1960s, a decade that was devoted to "little else but sex and rights—specifically, how to get more of each."[2] Since then, we've been swept along by an avalanche of collapsing moral standards. In some ways this process is best illustrated by the sexual behavior of a man named Gaetan Dugas, the airline steward who played a prominent role in spreading AIDS. In the decade before the disease burst upon the nation, Dugas averaged 250 sexual liaisons a year. In his words, "It's my right to do what I want with my body."[3] His "right," of course, cost him his life and lethally infected thousands of others. Individuals who insist on their "rights" rather than assuming the obligation to *do* right grease the cultural slide into a moral quagmire.

At the bottom of the slide, many think, we find ourselves held captive by barbarians—"new barbarians" who have emerged from our own ranks, threatening the very existence of Western civilization. Illustrating this, even high school students, Barbara Walters says, "have no sense of discipline. No goals. They care only for themselves. In short, they are becoming a generation of undisciplined cultural barbarians."[4]

Sociological data illustrate such moral anarchy. *The Day America Told the Truth*, a portrayal of this nation based upon extensive interviews, profiles a woman who worked as a prostitute for two years and is now married. One of her daughters, she suspects, was fathered by a man other than her husband—though neither her husband nor her daughter suspects this. The woman is unhappy with her marriage, uses drugs, admits she is bulimic, and has considered suicide.

She does, however, consider herself a "good, ethical person. On a 10-point scale from 'terrible' to 'great,' she gives herself a nine." Still more: "She is religious, a frequent churchgoer, absolutely certain of God's existence."[5] She no doubt believes in a God who loves her unconditionally, too gracious to hold her accountable before any bar of justice.

This woman illustrates the findings of a survey that reveals only one out of every three Christians believes his or her faith should shape one's lifestyle! Just *believe* that God *accepts* you just as you are, accept the fact that you are accepted, and then do whatever is acceptable to you! Even professed believers feel free to construct their own morality, removing the Ten Commandments from the walls of their hearts as well as the halls of our schools.

No wonder onlookers scoff at so-called Christians! Too many "believers" are like chubby physicians who tell their patients to lose weight—or aerobics instructors who sit in a chair, shouting amplified commands to the faithful fitness folks actually exercising. If the Christian Church is to recover its integrity, we who claim to be Christians must reclaim and proclaim some timeless truths, some moral *imperatives*, and walk rightly with God.

This issue, in a philosophical sense, stands revealed in Allan Bloom's *The Closing of the American Mind*, one of the most widely discussed treatises published in the past 25 years. Bloom wrote the book as "a meditation on the state of our souls, particularly those of the young, and their education."[6] Students need adult mentors to serve as midwives—helping them above all to deal with "*the* question, 'What is man?' in relation to his highest aspirations as opposed to his low and common needs."[7]

Today's students, Bloom says, are nice enough, even if unusually self-centered. Disinterested in the nature of human nature and lacking curiosity in grand, philosophical themes such as God, freedom, and immortality, today's youngsters think mainly about their own feelings and frustrations. They want to "discover themselves," to find some "self-esteem," to be "self-actualized," as preached by the psychogurus of our era.

Without *objective* standards, Bloom believes, we're awash in a pervasive ethical *relativism,* a philosophical dogma espoused by virtually everyone who enters or prowls about the university. Under the flag of "openness" and "tolerance" (while tolerating no *universal* truths or *traditional* values), folks freely follow their own feelings. As a Hemingway character contended: "Morality is in the eye of the beholder. So far, about morals, I know only that what is moral is what you feel good after and what is immoral is what you feel bad after."[8]

Such moral permissiveness, many Hemingway aficionados believe, constitutes a "free and democratic" society. To probe deeply into the reasons for this, Bloom digs for the philosophical roots of today's malaise and finds "nihilism, American style." It's an enormous intellectual earthquake that has shaken our culture to the foundations. It's *"the* most important and most astonishing phenomenon of our time," the "attempt to get 'beyond good and evil'" by substituting *"value* relativism" for Judeo-Christian absolutism.[9]

Bloom's critique finds support in Michael Novak's address "Awakening from Nihilism," a speech given when Novak accepted the prestigious Templeton Prize for Progress in Religion. "One principle that today's intellectuals most passionately disseminate is vulgar relativism," Novak says, "'nihilism with a happy face.' For them it is certain that there is no truth, only opinion: *my* opinion, *your* opinion." Consequently, "The most perilous threat to the free society today is, therefore, neither political nor economic. It is the poisonous, corrupting culture of relativism."[10]

Given this threat, Christ's Church must recover a moral source higher than the opinion polls and momentary personal feelings that prevail these days. It makes no more sense to consult public opinion on moral questions than it would to hold an election to determine the size of the Pacific Ocean or the highest peak in the Rocky Mountains. Moral standards resemble mountain ranges—they're majestically there, they're measurable, they have an arched pattern, and we ignore the unyielding absoluteness of their nature to our own discomfort or destruction. So we must intentionally point out and *teach* moral standards. This means pastors and parents and teachers must reclaim their rightful responsibilities, wresting them from television talk shows, movie stars, politicians, and street gangs.

It's time, in short, to recover and proclaim traditional Judeo-Christian moral standards, for time is running out! In significant ways, we've lost sight of those fixed stars of truth, which have forever guided mankind to the good life. This crisis of *moral* illiteracy overshadows other crises. We live in a society where many people lack any sense of propriety or civility and have minimal confidence in moral standards beyond their own personal preferences.

At the heart of this crisis, as Aleksandr Solzhenitsyn saw, is this: "Men have forgotten God."[11] This becomes clear as one examines various sinkholes in the cultural landscape—families, schools, media, government. Everywhere, it seems, there's a great vacuum regarding supernatural reality. By nature man craves a "Holy Other," an ultimate reason for being that gives the here and now meaning and direction. When God is shoved aside, embargoed from classrooms and courthouses, conscience evaporates and anarchy ensues.

Fortunately for us still rooted in the Christian tradition, there are some absolutes, some imperatives that have stood the test of time. The list was etched in stone, embedded in the Ten Commandments—10 rules to live by; 10 words to guide us; 10 ways to sustain a lasting, loving relationship with our Creator. Indeed, in the Jewish tradition, the day the commandments were given on Mount Sinai was often portrayed as a wedding day—a momentous event when binding vows were exchanged between two parties, which cemented a loving union. They are *10 steps to freedom*, for, as the psalmist rejoiced, "I will walk at liberty, for I seek Thy precepts" (Ps. 119:45, NASB).

Boundaries Create Freedom's Context

With the 10 Words in Exodus 20, the God who had delivered His people from slavery—the liberating Lord—set forth precepts and principles whereby folks keep covenant with Him. To know Yahweh, the ultimate, absolute Person, is to enjoy the freedom that grows out of fidelity, and this is the only bona fide liberty there is, the freedom that comes from living by vows. Real freedom emerges through self-discipline and integrity, through doing the truth, living in the truth.

Eight times in Exodus 20 the Lord begins a commandment with "You shall." Here we hear an *imperative* voice. He also said, "Remember" and "Honor," two more imperative verbs. Some things, He made clear, we must *do* to keep covenant with Him, our divine Lover. There are limits, parameters, to healthy, holy living.

All good things have boundaries. Our bodies, for example, have bone boundaries and skin boundaries. Were there no restraints on the cells and molecules of my bones, if every individual cell or molecule did its own thing, slipping and sliding wherever it pleased, I'd be a glob of jelly, unable to walk or hold hands with my wife. I'm free to move, free to experience the joys of life, because my bones have hard-and-fast boundaries, hard-and-fast edges.

Our skin, all nine pounds of it, provides a necessary boundary for our bodies. It's truly marvelous. In some areas, like the soles of our feet, it's tough; in other areas, like our lips, it's tender. It forms ridges on our fingers, uniquely ours, so that our fingerprints may be used to trace our identity. Most important, however, the skin is a restraining boundary, a definable limit to our body, keeping out what would injure us, keeping in what is vital for us. We're able to live freely because our skin keeps us together, firmly, in the place where we ought to be.

So I'm glad for my skin and bones—which, in my case, is about all there is to me! So too I'm glad for social and personal boundaries, which are necessary for the good life.

Increasingly, it seems, what was once disgraceful now elicits little condemnation. A popular Jewish rabbi, Manis Friedman, asks an important question with the title of his recent book: *Doesn't Anyone Blush Anymore?*[12] Some of us wonder today if there's anything truly off-limits or inappropriate. Are there real boundaries?

In truth, there *are* boundaries respected by mature persons. There are boundaries acknowledged by healthy men and women. If we're morally mature persons, we see how things truly are and act accordingly, doing the truth. The boundaries are in fact there for us to discover as responsible persons. Good relationships need boundaries, limits— yeas and nays, dos and don'ts.

Responsibilities Firm Up the Boundaries

When we accept responsibilities, we firm up the boundaries needed for good relationships, for a good life. This stands out clearly in an essay written by a college senior that appeared in *Newsweek*. He listed his laments, a series of complaints against his elders. Admittedly this generation of collegians have poorest Scholastic Aptitude Test (SAT) scores, know little geography or foreign languages, read very little, and are prisoners of fashionable fads. But, he claimed, "You did this to us. You prized your youth so much you made sure ours would be carefree." Parents *loved* their children and urged them to succeed and be happy. But they failed to teach them "to be responsible."[13]

This youngster illustrates what John Rosemond, a psychologist, predicted years ago when he spoke out against the so-called experts in his profession who were "promoting the entirely ludicrous idea that happiness and self-esteem go hand in hand." In fact, "Self-esteem and happiness are not one and the same. Keeping a child happy is as simple as giving the child everything he or she wants. That may prove expensive, but it's not difficult. Keeping a child happy takes less effort, less stamina, and certainly less courage than helping a child to grow up."

If parents keep a child "happy" for 18 years, Rosemond asserts, they will "completely destroy the child's self-esteem. Self-esteem, you see, is composed of equal parts initiative, resourcefulness, imagination, autonomy, and determination. Self-esteem is an attitude of 'I can do it myself.'" When parents fail to insist that children accept responsibility, when they try to keep them "happy" all the time, they keep them from growing up. Consequently, "When the time comes for these children to leave home and begin fending for themselves, many of them will not be prepared for self-sufficiency."[14]

That's tragic, for the key to personal dignity is the self-sufficiency that comes through taking responsibility, through accepting and carrying through obligations—in short, through self-discipline. To live well, to live maturely, to live freely demands self-discipline. Others may *force* us to do right, to be good, but only self-discipline, freely embraced, enables us to *be* righteous, to *be* good. Ultimately, self-discipline is moral: doing what's right because it's good.

An unattached guitar string is perfectly useless until you properly attach both ends of it to the guitar. You could pour a gallon of gasoline on the ground at the service station and light it (assuming no one stopped you), but it would just create a brief blazing bonfire. Only when you put it into your gas tank, routing it to your car's engine, where it explodes under tight restraints, does it serve your need for transportation. Only contained, restricted, disciplined explosions do productive work.

Relationships Demand the Limits of Self-discipline

And that, really, is what the Ten Commandments are all about. They are not endless rules with penalties for failure; they're 10 principles to live by, 10 ways to maintain fellowship with God, 10 words to be kept so as to behold His manifest presence, 10 boundaries to respect in order to nurture a loving union with our Maker. They are 10 steps to freedom!

Note that no threats accompany the commandments. God didn't say, "You shall not make graven images, because if you do, the next day a locomotive-sized meteorite will annihilate you." He didn't say, "You shall not commit adultery, for if you do, the next morning you'll be reduced to a glob of Silly Putty." No, He just spoke 10 Words—a recipe for living rightly with Him.

The Ten Commandments are a bit like guidelines for courteous courting. The only good reason for courting is to develop a good relationship with another person. Now I know some folks date for the wrong reasons—sexual thrills, ego satisfactions, free food. But those are just perversions of the only good reason for dating—to get to know another person.

Consequently, healthy dates have definable limits. Guys, if they're wise, don't try to date two women at the same time. Imagine trying to take two ladies to dinner at the same time, dashing from booth to booth, maintaining a meaningful conversation with both of them. Even the smoothest talking con man would surely fail to adequately entertain two women at the same time! By the end of the evening he would probably be stuffed with food, sitting in a booth all by himself.

What's true for dating is equally true for marriage. A woman out with her husband does well to keep her admiring eyes on him. If she continually inspects and favorably comments on the muscular physiques of every swaggering male, she'd lose her own man's ardor in short order! There are limits to how much you can notice others, to how much you can admire others, when you're in a loving relationship.

It's obvious: self-discipline—restricting ourselves to *one* person—establishes what we most long for: a loving relationship, a lasting union with a person. So, just as there are limits we must respect in courtships that mature into loving bonds, there are limits we must revere if we sustain any bond with God, the ultimate Person.

Rightly understood, God's commandments are not narrow restrictions meant to cramp our style. They are liberating steps, guiding us to the self-discipline basic to any lasting, loving relationship with a person. In this case, a divine Person, Yahweh, the Lord, seeks to draw us into a covenant bond, a lasting union, a spiritual marriage, with himself.

We who want to live with God have clear guidelines for doing right: the Ten Commandments. We need to grow up, to accept the freedom God has given us, and to take responsibility for our actions. We must remember, however, that these commandments were given us as ways whereby we consummate a covenant, not as edicts arbitrarily imposed to exact obedience. So it's important, before turning to the specifics of the Bible's legal code, to consider its context. Only in covenant can the Law be truly fulfilled. Only in covenant is the Law fully liberating. And only in the new covenant, consummated by Christ Jesus, is the Law truly liberating.

Such covenant theology underlies God's call to holy living. In an important recent encyclical, *The Splendor of Truth*, John Paul II sums up the Bible's call to holiness, personified in Jesus, incarnate Truth. In Christ we discover our calling

> to freedom in obedience to the divine law summarized in the commandment of love of God and neighbor. And this is what takes place through the gift of the Holy Spirit, the

Spirit of truth, of freedom and of love: in him we are enabled to interiorize the law, to receive it and to live it as
the motivating force of true personal freedom: "the perfect law, the law of liberty" (James 1:25 [RSV]).[15]

Jesus is the Light of the World. We who follow Him
walk in the light and, by obeying His Word, live holy lives.
Consequently, as we wonder how to decide what's right
and wrong, what's good and bad, we discover that Jesus
Christ is *the* Answer to all of humanity's deepest hunger
for truth. Thus, the Gospel account (Matt. 19:16) of the rich
young man who came to Jesus illuminates the entire human condition. The young man asked: "Teacher, what
good deed must I do to have eternal life?" (NRSV). All of us
ask that question, a fundamentally *moral* question, which
implicitly wonders about life's purpose, our final end.

Responding to the young man, Jesus reminded him
that "there is only one who is good" (v. 17, NRSV), God himself. Revering and serving God precedes all morality. Then
one rightly obeys His edicts—both the commandments inscribed in the natural law (rooted in God's eternal law)
and the divine Law revealed on Mount Sinai, which encap-
sulates the natural law. To that, one adds the righteous attitudes and motives prescribed in the Beatitudes, which enable one to follow Christ, who informs and gives substance
to Christian ethics.

Through the grace given us as believers, the presence
of the Holy Spirit enables us to live *conformed* to Christ's
likeness. Law and grace work together. "Faith working
through love" (Gal. 5:6, NASB) is the central formula, for it
enables us to "fulfill the law of Christ" (6:2, NASB). There's
a *synergy* to the Christlike life. Faith is more than mental
assent. It's a commitment, a devotion to a loving relationship with God through Christ, who is the Way, the Truth,
and the Life. This faith, totally trusting Him, opens our
hearts to His love, which in turn enables us to love Him
and our neighbor.

When we try to live under the Law, we seek comfort in grace; and with grace we find strength to live out the Law. Saved by grace through faith, we're enabled by the Holy Spirit to live out the new law, which incarnates—in our hearts—the statutes of Sinai.

Christ's Church, therefore, has one perennially compelling commission: to bring persons to Jesus. By preaching the gospel, by bringing sinners to salvation, by affording them means of grace, they are given the opportunity—the birthright of believers—to live righteously. The high standards of Christian morality are for Christians, men and women willingly transformed by the supernatural workings of God's grace. Such is possible only for free moral agents, so freedom must be treasured in order for morality to exist. But it is in fact possible to live rightly, for God does not command us to do what we cannot do.

Consequently, there are various behaviors that are clearly right and others that are manifestly wrong. Just as there are clearly defined rules in a game of baseball, there is an objective reality to moral acts that makes them intrinsically right or wrong. This eliminates various personal opinions and calculating ethical judgments, for Christians ought never to focus solely on the bottom-line consequences of their acts.

God has called us to live rightly, pleasing Him as we allow Him to conform us to Christ. Salvation full and free moves beyond forgiveness of sins. Christ's redemption, says John Paul II, grants us "the possibility of realizing the *entire truth* of our being," the freedom from sin's bondage for which we are fundamentally designed.[16]

In the covenant's consummation there is freedom. Redeemed through the grace of God, we are set free to live in accord with the plan of our Master, Christ Jesus our Lord.

2

The Covenant Context

God Is Present

By nature we are social beings. Designed to live in community, we shun isolation, sensing the ultimate anguish of solitary confinement. Yet from the moment of our birth, wrenched from the womb, we struggle with the anxiety that comes from separation, from the aloneness that marks a new creature. In truth, we live and die individually; we can never fully escape the shell of our particularity. So there is an inescapable, aching aloneness, like the emptiness of Carlsbad Caverns, carved into the heart of the human condition. Like death, it opens for us a window on reality, the ultimate issues of life, for at the Judgment we'll each be judged as a particular person, not as a digit in a crowd, as a worker bee whose identity is yoked to the queen.

Still, it's painful to be alone! In the deepest level of our souls, when they ache, there is an empty space. Throughout life, for a variety of reasons we feel lonely. It's obviously the lonely who sing the songs, crowd the singles' bars, and giggle through the "happy hours." Only the lonely—and that's most of us at times—know the pains of separation, isolation, the feeling of being unknown and unwanted. Most deeply, there's an existential void felt by all who are estranged from God. In our hearts we feel W. H. Auden's truth:

> *Faces along the bar*
> *Cling to the average day;*
> *The lights must never go out,*
> *The music must always play*
> *Lest we know where we are,*
> *Lost in a haunted wood,*
> *Children afraid of the dark*
> *Who have never been happy or good.*[1]

What's the Matter? A Matter of Facelessness!

Loneliness, of course, has little to do with being alone. Solitude uniquely restores and refreshes us. We often need time alone, time to be by ourselves, to be ourselves; we need interludes of reflection and contemplation. Amazingly, we are loneliest in a crowd, surrounded by faceless faces, unknown by unknowns, unwanted and unnamed.

That's because we hunger for more than crowds of faceless folks, even when they applaud us. We hunger for a face that assures us we're real and have worth, that we amount to something, that we literally weigh something, like a rock on a scale, that we matter. We long for an affirmation of our own authenticity, of substance, a confirmation of our dignity as persons. In a crowd of faceless faces, we long for a face that knows us and acknowledges our standing as persons.

Living in San Diego, I sometimes see televised reports of sailors returning home after months at sea. The camera first shows hundreds of them peering intently toward the shore. Next it shows hundreds of women and children peering toward the ship. Then, at magical moments, the faces light up. Men see their wives; wives spot their husbands. The face is recognized; the person is present to the eye. With recognition comes transformation, for faces that strained to see suddenly fill with life when they see their beloved.

What Matters: Faces

Loneliness, isolation ends when we see a face we know, a face that knows us. Faces, you see, are *peculiar*. Just study the peculiarity of the face of the next person you meet. Some of you perhaps feel offended, for sometimes we think "peculiar" means strange or odd, but that's not the root meaning of the word. "Peculiar" means distinctive and unique, belonging to one person. It's one of the majesties of creation that every face is unique, that every face is peculiarly one person's.

Consider, for example, how differently we see elbows. I've seen lots of elbows in my life, but not one of them has proved memorable. I doubt that I'd be able to pick out my wife's elbows in a lineup of them! One elbow is pretty much like any other one to me. If you've seen one, you've seen them all.

But faces are memorable. Most of us remember (or at least claim we remember) faces better than names. That's because faces are *peculiar,* unique, and distinctive, more so than names. The first thing most of us notice when we see another person is his or her face, for faces are revealing.

Our faces reveal our ancestry. Yet there's a sense in which we also shape our faces. Each of us helps carve the wrinkles and crinkles, form the muscles and flesh, the body that bears witness to our being. Our experiences, our choices leave traces on our faces. The wisdom of age lines the creases and wrinkles of saintly faces. A senior citizen's facial lines often reveal either dissipation or discipline, wasteful diversions or wise devotions. (One lady, however, asked an understandable question: "If God had to give a woman wrinkles, why couldn't He put them on her feet instead of on her face?")

Most important, faces reveal *presence.* The strangers I meet on sidewalks, strangers whose eyes rarely meet mine, aren't really present to me. Consequently, they aren't really real. When someone I know turns his or her back on me, hides his or her face from me, that person withholds his or her presence. But when I recognize a person—and when that person recognizes me—there's *presence*. That's what we long for—the presence of a person who affirms our being, our "being there to him or her," the presence of a person who stands out from his or her surroundings, the presence of a person who confirms our standing, the reality of our being and worth.

The Glory of His Presence

One of the great revelations of Scripture, perhaps the most basic and central truth of the Judeo-Christian faith, is this: *God is present. He's here. He presents himself as a present to us.* That revelation, that truth permeates one of the greatest books ever written, the Book of Exodus. The central message of the book, when it's read as a whole, declares that Yahweh is always and everywhere with His people. That message leaps from the pages of chapter 3, where we find Moses herding his father-in-law's sheep. He "led the flock to the far side of the desert and came to Horeb, the mountain of God. There the angel of the LORD appeared to him in flames of fire from within a bush" (vv. 1-2).

His curiosity piqued, Moses checked it out. Then the Lord spoke from within the bush, "Moses! Moses!" So Moses said, "Here I am." Then God said, "Do not come any closer. . . . Take off your sandals, for the place where you are standing is holy ground" (vv. 4-5). At this, Moses hid his face, fearing to face Yahweh. At that point God told Moses He planned to rescue the children of Israel and give them a promised land. Still more: Moses was to lead them! The Lord assured him, saying, "I will be with you" (v. 12). Needing still more assurance, however, Moses wondered what to say if his people asked, "What is his name?" And "God said to Moses, 'I AM WHO I AM'" (vv. 13-14).

In this marvelous moment, what we call a "theo-phany" (God's self-disclosure), Moses sensed the manifest presence of God. God offered him His best present: His presence. The Hebrew language uses the same word for both *presence* and *face*. On the slopes of Mount Horeb Moses encountered God. He's the One who is, the God with a face, the One who always has been and always will be, the One who is always and everywhere with us and for us.

In a way, the world and our experience in it resemble one of those picture puzzles I pondered as a child. There was a picture that looked like a jungle, full of trees and vines; if you studied it, you'd suddenly see the images of a lion, then a giraffe, then an elephant, then a big-game hunter. Suddenly the picture clearly revealed curiously concealed images within it. And that's our world: a visible sign of an invisible reality, a visible puzzle containing an elusive image. It's a world filled with the presence of a Per-son, the One who is.

So God is always with us. As Augustine said, God "abides forever, for whose presence there is no waiting, and of whose absence there is no fear, because, by the very fact that He truly *is*, He is always present."[2] At times we all feel a bit like Moses, herding sheep, alone on an isolated mountainside. We may have turned our backs on Him, sought to ignore Him while doing our own thing, or failed to see Him as He is. But we're hungry for a face we know, a face that knows us. The good news from God's Word for all of us is this: whatever our situation, however dismal our predicament, God is present. He's right here with us.

Rightly approached, everything we touch touches on the eternally real, the one Lord of all, whose being sustains all beings. The One who is, Yahweh, comes to us, as He came to Moses, in the midst of our ordinary routines, sud-denly speaking from a common bush. But most of us are so wrapped up in ourselves, so absorbed in our problems and fantasies, that we fail to see the burning bushes on the slopes of our lives. As Elizabeth Barrett Browning wrote,

> *Earth's crammed with heaven,*
> *And every common bush afire with God;*
> *But only he who sees takes off his shoes—*
> *The rest sit round it and pluck blackberries.*[3]

In your world, in my world, God is here. For He is. He's the only One who is simply the great "I AM." He's the One in whom "we live and move and have our being" (Acts 17:28). And He longs to present himself, to be present to us, to reveal to us His manifest presence.

Christian faith is a gift from God. It's a divine gift, a present. It's a gift of God's here-and-now reality, His living presence. And He would like to give us that gift if we would but turn aside and pause to see Him.

A Covenanting God—a Covenant People

During the late 1960s, to justify American involvement in Vietnam, United States President Lyndon Baines Johnson declared we had a moral obligation, because of treaties we had signed, to defend South Vietnam. Treaties, he said, are like sacred vows—and America has never broken its treaty agreements.

At that point thousands of American Indians fell out of their chairs in laughter. (My Cherokee-Sioux ancestry may be injecting some biases here!) Indians have good memories. They've kept track of the treaties made—and broken—by the United States. As a bumper sticker says, "Broken Treaty Score: Whites 398; Indians 0." No contest!

Much of the tragedy of American Indian history lies rooted in the reality of broken treaties, broken promises, broken vows. And much of the tragedy of human history unravels amid the reality of broken treaties, broken promises, broken vows. In international relations, in human relations, in divine-human relations, one of the enduring evils (endemic to our species) is the persistence of broken promises. It's the way the world turns. Sadly enough, there's an accuracy to the jaded cynicism of the French soldier-statesman Charles de Gaulle, who rightly compared treaties with roses and pretty young girls: "They last," he said, "while they last."[4]

Yet we humans have the unique ability to make promises. We do so continually. And we rely on promises. Promises sustain us as surely as oxygen. Without promises we can't be human. Nothing gives us more hope, more comfort, than their expected fulfillment. Conversely, nothing devastates us more completely than broken promises, broken vows. So it ought not surprise us, when we turn to Holy Scripture, to find that the God who is really present makes promises. He's a promise-making, covenanting God. And He wants to draw us into a covenant bond with himself.

The Terms: God's Ways with His World

In the 19th chapter of Exodus we find Moses and the Israelites, just liberated from slavery in Egypt, encamped in front of Mount Sinai—in the same area where Moses had earlier encountered the Lord Yahweh in the burning bush and had glimpsed the reality of His manifest presence. Now, leading his people, Moses needed God's guidance. On the mountain the Lord reminded Moses of His holy acts, having delivered Israel from bondage. Then He called them to "obey me fully and keep my covenant," so as to enjoy His presence and His world, wherein they would be for Him "a kingdom of priests and a holy nation" (vv. 5-6).

In this episode God extended His covenant to the children of Israel. The covenant message first announced to Noah, then to Abraham, then to Moses, is here extended to the Israelites at Mount Sinai. Such a covenant in the ancient world was a political agreement, cemented by vows of lasting fidelity—much like those in King Arthur's medieval English court that bound knights and their lords. God offered the Israelites—and through them to us, their spiritual heirs—a real deal. It was not a "square deal" or a "new deal" or a "fair deal," but a *real deal!*

Many of us have difficulty with the ancient idea of covenant because we've been soured by politicians and political deals. We're pretty confident God would never resemble the politicians we know whose words rarely ring true. If even part of what candidates for office say about each other is true, none of them deserve to be elected! Most of what politicians promise we instinctively disbelieve, for it seems they spend half their time making promises and the other half making up excuses as to why they can't keep their promises.

But God's covenant, though detailed in treaty terms, offers more than political promises. God offered Israel a real deal: the reality of His presence. He promised to be with them, to lead them to the Promised Land. He promised to enable them to become what He had planned for them from the beginning: His children.

In exchange for His faithfulness, His present presence, God asked His people to be faithful, to respond to Him. So He offers himself to us, as brides and grooms offer themselves to one another, through a covenant, through freely given promises. Later on in Israel's history, when the prophets spoke of covenant, they used the symbol of marriage, rather than of treaties, to illustrate God's ways with His people. We understand that married men and women, when asked what they most desire in their spouse, reply, "Fidelity."

Marriage, rightly entered, is a covenant, not a contract. We're more familiar with contracts, of course. When we buy cars or take out loans or accept jobs, we sign contracts. They briefly bind us together to secure some mutually profitable objective, for we sign contracts to secure short-term gains. Rarely do we much care about the personal rapport established by a contract. Business contracts have worth, but they are inevitably expedient. So if we try to establish personal relationships through contracts, we court disaster. When people marry in a contractual fashion, they rarely stay married.

Covenants, however, unite persons differently than contracts. Covenants bind together people who want lasting, loving relationships, not personal dividends. Covenants unite persons who acknowledge their differences, their inequalities, who seek to give rather than get, who sense a sacred dimension to the vows they take, knowing they deal with permanent, eternal realities. And through Moses, on the sacred mountain, Mount Sinai, the Lord entered into a covenant with His people. He made promises designed to last eternally.

Several years ago Robertson McQuilkin resigned his position as president of Columbia Bible College and Seminary. He did so to devote himself full-time to caring for Muriel, his wife of 42 years, then stricken with Alzheimer's disease. Though some well-intending friends urged him to place her in a health-care institution so that he might continue his important ministry, he decided his first calling was not to ministry but to marriage. He then devoted each day to caring for her, as a parent must care for a small child. He found, despite the discomfort, that "Muriel is the joy of my life. Daily I discern new manifestations of the kind of person she is, the wife I always loved. I also see fresh manifestations of God's love—the God I long to love more fully."[5]

That's what we mean by "covenant"—fidelity!

The Blood Covenant-Monument

If you come to my San Diego townhouse, you'll find at the front door an old-fashioned school desk with a little chalkboard on the wall behind it that bears the inscription: "RKS + GAR—Welcome to the Reeds'." The initials stand for Roberta Kay Steininger and Gerard Alexander Reed. They identify the couple who dwell there.

Whenever we make promises, we seem drawn—almost instinctively—to inscribe them on monuments, drawing symbols of personal vows that remind us that we are participants in the reality of covenant. Later, if we break our covenants, we usually demolish the monuments earlier raised. After a divorce, former lovers often take their wedding bands and hock them, or they get a jeweler to reshape the diamonds and gold into something—anything—other than a symbol of wedlock.

Living covenants, binding promises, prompt us to build monuments to enshrine or sanctify them. When we marry, something more than convention impels us to have wedding ceremonies, for marriage means more than living together. Marriage testifies to a hunger for *permanence*. A wedding formalizes two persons' intention to sink the foundation of their love to bedrock, something deeper than the waves of life. Years ago a couple married atop the Rock of Gibraltar; the groom explained, "We chose the site because we wanted to found our marriage on a rock." Good decision!

We try to *symbolize* something in a wedding, something that transcends the routine agreements we make with friends and business associates. Ceremonies point to realities. When we make promises, we want to make them public, to sanctify them somehow by including witnesses who know the truth about our vows. We literally long to etch our promises into concrete as evidence of the permanence of our commitment.

Similarly God, in the process of extending His covenant to His people, established a monument—a visible symbol—to stand forever, a witness to it. He set up an altar, a blood-bathed monument, to His life-giving commitment to man.

The Monument: a Blood-Bathed Altar

Having announced the covenant in Exodus 19, God revealed to Moses its contents in chapter 20: the Ten Commandments, guides to the good life, responding with love to God's love, forming a lasting, loving relationship with Him. Then, in chapter 24, God revealed through a dramatic symbol the enduring *means* by which we keep the covenant.

Moses, we read, "built an altar at the foot of the mountain" (v. 4). Here they "sacrificed young bulls" (v. 5). Then Moses "took the Book of the Covenant and read it to the people," who said, "We will do everything the LORD has said; we will obey" (v. 7). Then he "took the blood, sprinkled it on the people and said, 'This is the blood of the covenant that the LORD has made with you'" (v. 8).

Altars stand at the center of Israel's life and of life itself. More than 400 times in the Old Testament we find altars constructed—altars that physically represent God's covenant with His people. Unlike the mythical speculations of some religions, Israel's faith had rock-hard substance. God's promises to Noah, to Abraham, to Moses took physical form in altars. Moses made altars of earth or unhewn stones, using the earth's natural materials rather than humanly designed artworks. If we remember that Exodus proclaims the reality of God's presence, it's clear that anywhere there is earth and stone, we can build altars to commemorate His presence.

If we fail to build altars appropriate to God, we turn like the ancient people of Babel to building altars to sun and moon or various facets of ourselves. For we worship what we esteem or admire. Whatever we consider *most worthy* becomes the object of our religion, for religion is the means whereby we try to retie the inner bond with reality that we sense has been broken. Human nature is as indelibly religious as it is nutritional. We may choose to eat Hostess Twinkies or whole wheat biscuits—but we will eat! Just as we can eat right things or wrong things, so too we can worship the right Person or the wrong persons.

Our society abounds with misguided worshipers, men

and women giving worth and life service to less than ultimate ends. Years ago I asked a class of students to list the
things they most wanted to learn in life. Many responded
by saying they most wanted to know how to live happily,
how to love rightly, how to enjoy God forever. One student, that year's star basketball player, took another tack.
He wanted, he said, to know how to shoot a basketball better, to pass a basketball better, to dribble a basketball better,
to maneuver a basketball down the court and into the
hoop somehow. Nothing else in life concerned him. In his
world, *success* rolled with a ball to a hoop. And "success"
has always been an object of worship. Ancient peoples
erected statues celebrating the gods and goddesses of success—just as our success gods and goddesses routinely
grace television and magazine advertisements.

To worship, we build appropriate places. Many modern buildings—banks, office complexes, sports arenas—address deeply religious desires. Throngs of concertgoers often seek some sort of spiritual comfort. Years ago on
television I saw a man interviewed who was deeply dis-
tressed that he had not received the seats he sought at a
Neil Diamond concert. This man had stood in line for
hours to buy the tickets he thought would get him close to
the stage. When asked why it was so important to be close
to Neil Diamond, he said: "My brother died last summer,
and I just had to hear Neil sing 'He Ain't Heavy—He's My
Brother.'"

This man may never go to church, but he needs to find
some way to cope with death, so he goes to a concert! It's a
place of worship, a place with an altar. Such shrines,
modernity's altars, say much about us. Tragically, future
generations may be appalled at our tawdry shrines, our
tinsel altars. In the words of T. S. Eliot, "Here were decent
godless people; Their only monument the asphalt road and
a thousand lost golf balls."[6]

Covenant Altars, Where Blood Is Shed

Our secular altars lack power because they lack life. They celebrate tinsel-toned illusions. They promote distractions. They evade life's deepest realities. But the altars erected in the Bible had blood on them. That's why they were built. They absorbed the blood that was splashed on them.

Because we understand blood's life-giving power, we understand its spiritual symbolism. When we want to express lasting friendship, we call someone a "blood brother." There is power in blood. And there is power in the symbols associated with blood. In the Old Testament covenant, the blood poured on the altar signified God's extended, enduring forgiveness. The blood sprinkled on the people represented their willingness to obey the Lord, to uphold the covenant.

We humans need forgiveness. We also long for something, or Someone, to give ourselves to. We want to surrender—to obey—not out of fear, but to claim the promises. We can deal with the past only with forgiveness, and we can face the future only with hopes rooted in promise. To deal with the past, we must forgive; to face the future, we must be capable of making and keeping promises. Forgiveness frees us for life.

There's a story of a man who threw a rock at a stray dog to chase it away. He threw more accurately, more forcefully, than he had intended and hit the dog, breaking its leg. Instead of running away, however, the dog limped back and licked his hand. "That day," he said, "I truly understood the meaning of God's unfailing love." In truth, the Bible declares, God is merciful. He forgives! And that eternal truth took form in a monument, a testament, on altars, where the innocent blood of animals was spilled to atone for human sins.

The Promise Perfected: a New Covenant

The discomfort of aging results not from the fact that time passes quickly, but that it lumbers its way so slowly through pointless routines. We do the same things—the same old things—over and over again. We get up. We go to work. We come home and go to bed. We've done it mechanically, measuring out our lives, as T. S. Eliot said, with coffee spoons. Yet the routines grow progressively more meaningless. We who are not old fear old age, I suspect, not only because the end of life draws near, but also because we fear we'll have to admit we've never truly lived.

When empty routines drive our days, time's a drag, life's a bore. If we're paralyzed by the past, if we're passé about the future, each day brings us little more than toast and tea—and we measure out our lives with coffee spoons.[7] Yet we really don't want that. We don't want to be bystanders, growing old with nothing to show for it but wrinkled coats and yellowed social security checks. In fact, few of us want to grow old. Since we love life, we fear the loss of life that old age implies.

Some good things, we know, need refurbishing, reviving. They age, they become old, but they are too valuable to discard. They need to be remade, overhauled, and made new. If you break your arm, for instance, you don't need an arm transplant—you need the fracture fixed. And the reset bone, wonder of wonders, will mend so as to make the broken spot stronger than ever. Life, however much we enjoy it, inexorably runs down. Its brokenness needs mending. We need a transcendent remaking, a recovery of our true life: our image-of-God life.

The New Covenant

It's in this sense that we Christians understand the old covenant as enunciated in the Hebrew Scriptures. We are indeed people of a new covenant; but the old covenant, one of the central components of Israel's faith, remains embedded in the new. The very division of the Bible—Old and New Testaments—reveals that fusion, for we root our faith in both the Hebrew and Christian Scriptures. We do so because we believe the New Testament is like a seed in the pod of the Old Testament, and the Old Testament flowers forth in the New. They fit together like tongue-and-groove flooring.

This theme helps shape the Book of Hebrews, one of the most profound New Testament letters, the Christian text that deals most thoroughly with the new covenant. Outlining how Jesus perfectly fulfills the Old Testament law, Hebrews portrays Jesus as the consummate High Priest, doing once and forever what no purely human priest had been able to do, conclusively establishing the new covenant. The old covenant needed something more: it needed an overhaul; the broken bone needed resetting. As we read in Hebrews 8, the new covenant promises full forgiveness, making "obsolete" (v. 13) the old.

The Old Covenant (as Promised) Perfected

The old covenant was largely external and performance based. There were commandments, formal obligations that sustained the God-Israel bond. Yet doing things just because we're told to do them always leaves something to be desired, something lacking in a relationship.

I'm glad, growing up in church, that I never smoked cigarettes, though in those days it was "cool" for adolescents (aping movie stars) to do it. Then, in 1964, the United States surgeon general declared cigarette smoking injurious to one's health, and the church's stance made more sense. The rule was rooted in *truth*—truth about reality. Not smoking keeps one healthy! I was able then to explain that I didn't smoke, not simply because the church said it was wrong, but because it's unwise to court suicide! What I had done as a child, out of obedience, I do now as an adult—freely, joyously, thankfully.

Similarly, the people of God had a relationship with Him under the old covenant. But they frequently failed to uphold their half of the agreement; they failed to obey His

Law. So something new was needed. The old needed re-
newing, and that meant the Law needed to become an inner principle, freely followed because fully embraced and
as active as yeast in one's heart and mind.

Still more: the new covenant provided the intimacy
between God and man so necessary for vital spirituality.
Under the old covenant, people learned *about* God through
teachers, like biology students studying human anatomy
in textbooks. Under the new covenant we can actually
know God as husbands and wives know each other—inti-
mately. We can enter into, become one with, know God
through personal *communion.*

We long for personal intimacy. We're profoundly sexual persons, yet our deepest hunger is for intimacy. What
we want, in sexual bonding—the *conjugal* act—is more
than pleasure. We crave an intimacy that lasts longer than
an ecstatic moment, though we often lack the courage to
reveal our inner selves so as to establish real intimacy with
another person.

And that's exactly what God seeks to establish in the
new covenant, effected by Jesus Christ for us. This new
life, this new covenant, comes to us through God's gracious forgiveness. Partially available under the old covenant through yearly rituals, full forgiveness forms the basis
of the new covenant. Solely because He loves us, God in
Christ has forgiven us.

In fact, He forgives and forgets. Now that's forgiveness! When we humans forget something, it's usually a
mark of weakness rather than strength. Forgetfulness dis-
tinguishes the senile—or the absent-minded professors
among us. Marilyn Monroe was a celebrated actress, but
she had trouble remembering her lines. While filming *Some
Like It Hot,* she repeatedly forgot the script for a certain
scene. Finally, on the 53rd take, director Billy Wilder put the
lines on pieces of paper in every drawer of a bureau; Mon-

roe was to go to the bureau, pull out the drawer, and see her lines. With everything set, the cameras whirled—and Monroe went to the wrong chest of drawers! We do forget.

But God's forgetfulness comes from His omnipotence—He's strong enough to forget our transgressions. When we accept His promises, when we embrace His offer of salvation, when we allow His Son, Jesus, access to our hearts, when we bare our souls in contrition and repentance, God thoroughly, totally forgives us for Christ's sake.

You who work with computers know that you can have literally millions of bits of information stored on a disk; then by striking one key (whether intentionally or not), that data will totally disappear. It was once there, but now it's forever gone! It's as if the information was never there. There is new storage space on the disk. So it is with God's ability to forgive. He washes away our sins, and from His standpoint they are simply gone, forgotten because they are no longer part of us.

The grace of God's forgiveness, the promise of His forgetfulness, extends to us today. It's the new covenant, established not by the animal sacrifices of the old covenant, but by the internalized intimacy and freeing forgiveness brought to us by the new covenant.

To Perfect the Promise: Give God *Agapē!*

Many of us at times feel we're born losers. But we're not! We may choose to lose, but we're not born to lose. We are, however, born to love. We're born lovers. If we're alive, we're lovers. So the question is not *"Will* we love?" but *"What* will we love?" *"How* will we love?" and *"How well* will we love what we love?" The right ordering of love stands at the center of covenant theology, for our response to the God of love who invites us into covenant is the response of love.

To indicate the kinds of things we love, the English language prefixes the Greek word *philo* to whatever it is

that we love. Most of us are fine *philautists*—we love ourselves. I've noticed numbers of *philogynists* at the college
where I teach—men who have a certain fondness for
women. Some of you are *philobrutists*—you love animals;
perhaps you've even lavishly appropriated funds for your
pets in your wills. Lots of ladies display *philocoma*—the
love of hair. And a few men (often balding men, I've noticed) become *philopogonists*—lovers of beards. There are
philanthropists (lovers of humanity) and musicians with
philharmonic tastes. There are *philosophers*, who profess to
love wisdom. There are *philatelists*, who love stamps so
much that they invest much of their lives and earnings col-
lecting them. Clearly, we love lots of things. And we love
them in various ways.

The Greek language is a finely nuanced, precise language. Whereas we have only one word "love," which
must be variously used and its meaning determined by its
context, the Greeks (and thus the writers of the New Testament) deployed several words to clearly indicate their intent. In the Bible the word *agapē*, meaning godly love, signifies the highest form of love: it's a benevolent, unselfish
commitment to another's well-being. It's the basic reality
of the universe—and it's the principal ingredient of scrip-
tural holiness.

Great Danish thinker Søren Kierkegaard titled one of
his books *Purity of Heart Is to Will One Thing*. I want to set
forth a corollary to that statement and declare: "Holiness of
heart is to love one God." In essence, holiness is the singular will to love God above all else.

When Jesus said the greatest commandment is to *love*
God, He used the word *agapē*. In Mark 12 a scribe asked
Him, "Which is the first commandment of all?" (v. 28, KJV).
Jesus said: "The first of all the commandments is, Hear, O
Israel; the Lord our God is one Lord: and thou shalt love
the Lord thy God with all thy heart, and with all thy soul,

and with all thy mind, and with all thy strength" (vv. 29-30, KJV).

To formulate our understanding of *agapē*, let's use the letters of the word mnemonically, indicating how it brings together and perfects all that's good in love. *agapē* is, I think, (1) **a**ttentive, (2) **g**rateful, (3) **a**vailable, (4) **p**ersuaded, and (5) **e**ternal.

Agapē **is attentive**. To love God, we must give Him more than a passing glance. Love, as routinely as a revolving door, turns to face its beloved. "One thing have I desired of the LORD," David said, "that will I seek after; that I may dwell in the house of the LORD all the days of my life, to behold the beauty of the LORD, and to inquire in his temple" (Ps. 27:4, KJV). *Agapē* attends to God, notices Him, gives Him a lingering look.

Rightly attentive, love is aware of whatever or whoever it loves. Attention is one of love's ligaments, running like a strong strand of muscle through it; and attention directed to God wraps itself in the form of prayer. Prayer is attending to, or being attentive to, God. In fact, Simone Weil insists, love has "attention for its substance." And since *"prayer* consists of attention," we love God by giving Him our attention, our prayer-full attention. If you *agapaō* (the verb form of *agapē*) God, you give Him more than a glance, you give Him your attention. You pray.

Agapē **is grateful**. Lovers spontaneously praise their loved ones. They are moved to joy simply by the sheer *being* of their beloved. They are delighted with them just for being what they *are*. So David declared, "Bless the LORD, O my soul: and all that is within me, bless his holy name" (Ps. 103:1, KJV).

Grateful lovers acknowledge their debts, admit their dependencies, give thanks for others' goodness. Often we fail to notice things until they are gone, fail to notice other's kindnesses until they are gone—things like Mom's cooking!

(I talked once with a college girl who was a bit homesick. What she missed most, she said, was her mom's cooking. Her friend felt the same way about her own homesickness, adding, "And my mom's not even a good cook!")

A woman got onto a crowded bus. Obviously exhausted, she reached up to take hold of the overhead bar, since all the seats were taken, when a man offered her his seat. Totally shocked at such chivalry, the woman fainted. After she revived and took the offered seat, she thanked the man—at which point *he* fainted! Gratitude, it seems, does not flood the world. We're so tempted to think we're making it on our own that we fail to notice how often others help us. Sometimes it takes a shock of some sort to jolt us into gratitude.

But *agapē* needs no jolts. *Agapē* takes notice and gives thanks. *Agapē* praises God, the God from whom all blessings flow. *Agapē* simply praises as it goes.

***Agapē* is available.** Lovers somehow find time for one another. Lovers eagerly wait upon, wait for, do things with, and do things for the one they love. We're literally at the *disposal* of the ones we love. So John said, "Love means living the way God commanded us to live" (2 John 6, NCV).

A state forester, checking boundary lines in an isolated area of northern California, walked up a dirt road to find the landowner of a homestead adjoining state property. At the gate he found signs: Private Property—No Trespassing! Along the path other signs declared, Keep Out—This Means You! and Beware of Dog! Having a job to do, the forester pressed on to the cabin, where he met and talked with the property owner, who turned out to be unusually talkative and friendly. His mission accomplished, the forester prepared to leave, and the landowner kept talking. Finally, needing to get on with his work, the forester reached the door, and the landowner said: "Come and see me again sometime. I don't get many visitors up this way."[8]

Too many of us have Private Property—No Trespassing! signs nailed on the gateposts of our lives. Keep Out—This Means You! rather leaps from our countenances. Some of us even have Beware of God signs! But love takes down such signs. Love makes me available to my beloved, moves me to offer him or her my life, molds me in service to the one I love.

Agapē is **persuaded**. Love carries its own assurance, knows some things for sure. Thus Paul declared: "I am persuaded, that neither death, nor life . . . nor any other creature, shall be able to separate us from the love of God, which is in Christ Jesus our Lord" (Rom. 8:38-39, KJV).

There's a *certainty* to love. Lots of things about God I don't really understand. At times I wish He would dramatically reveal himself to me—perhaps by making me the next winner of a $10 million sweepstakes. Yet though many things are unknown, faith in God is not accepting some scientific or philosophical theorem. It's falling in love with Jesus. And you *can* know you're in love. You *can* know when you are loved. There is a certainty to it all. Love is persuaded.

There is also a *confidence* in love. It's amazing how hopeful you become when you fall in love. Love breeds confidence. Love nurtures hope. A noted psychologist says people tend to see life as either a problem or a privilege. Well, lovers rejoice in life's privileges. They walk confidently into an unknown future because they walk hand in hand with someone they trust. So *agapē* is persuaded.

Agapē is **eternal**. The ad that declares "Diamonds Are Forever" exaggerates, though diamonds will last longer than a new Rolls-Royce, the current best-selling novel, or the latest rock-and-roll star. We're drawn to diamonds, I suspect, as a symbol for love, because we have a deep longing for forever, for a love that lasts, that lasts forever. Thus the psalmist says, "Lord, you have been our dwelling place throughout all generations. Before the mountains were born or you brought forth the earth and the world, from everlasting to everlasting you are God" (90:1-2). In our hearts we know that love, when it's real, is forever.

In the summer of 1980 a young lady was stabbed seven times and strangled to death in her Miami apartment. She was 38, had a good job, and lived the "swinging single" life. In the words of a bumper sticker, she was a "party animal." She seemed to live the "good life" portrayed in television soaps and ads. But in death she left a diary that disclosed that under the facade of a party animal was a lonely person. She had had 59 lovers in the final 56 months of her life.

Yet she confessed in her diary: "I would like to have . . . once before I pass through my life the kind of a sexual relationship that is part of a loving relationship." Still more: "I'm alone," she wrote, "and I want to share something with somebody."[9] This young lady longed for a love that lasts. We all long for a love that lasts—eternally. We long for eternal love; we long for God. We want *Agapē*, Love itself.

What does God want from us? How do we respond to His offered covenant? That's simple! *Give Me* agapē, *says He!* Such love comes from the God who is love. We can love God, we can give Him *agapē*, when we allow Him—*Agapē* itself—to fill us.

The one thing that makes us holy, the one thing that counts for eternity, the one thing God desires of a man or woman, is *agapē*. Such love comes into focus when we reflect on the Ten Commandments, the 10 Words given to Moses on Mount Sinai shortly after the deliverance of the Israelites from Egyptian bondage. Their newly discovered freedom, their newly discerned opportunity to enter into a covenant relationship with Yahweh gained substance and direction from the commandments inscribed on a stone tablet. So having stressed the importance of covenant, the context for the commandments, we now turn to a study of the Ten Commandments, considering both their Old and New Testament implications, in an effort to understand how then we should live.

PART TWO

Ten Steps
to Freedom

3

A Sacred Trust

OLD TESTAMENT FOUNDATION: NO OTHER GODS

In 1980 Bob Dylan received a Grammy award for "Best Male Rock Vocal Performance." The evening's climax, in many observers' minds, came when Dylan, greeted by a standing ovation, strode to the stage and sang "Gonna Have to Serve Somebody."

Dylan's right. You're gonna have to serve somebody! I'm gonna have to serve somebody. It's true. We choose whom or what we serve—but we can't choose *not* to serve.

Life is ultimately a matter of worship. We live according to what we think matters. We worship what we ultimately esteem or admire. That to which we attribute worth we worship. What we consider most worthy becomes the formative focus of our religion. In his *Larger Catechism*, Martin Luther declared that whatever our hearts embrace and trust becomes our God.

In its religious expressions we seek, in a multitude of often complex and bizarre ways, to retie the bond with reality that we sense has been severed. The Latin root of the word *religare* means "to tie back," so when we feel "at loose ends," we try to reconnect things. We're simply born with a longing for ultimate reality, a reality that religion seeks to fulfill.

As human beings we're both spiritual and physiological. We may eat sugar cookies or whole wheat bread—but we will eat something. We may choose to breathe carbon monoxide in a closed garage or pure air in the Rocky Mountains—but we will breathe something. We may serve the devil, or we may serve the Lord—but we will serve somebody; we will worship something. But *only one* person, the Bible says, really deserves our worship: Yahweh, the Lord.

Yahweh Our Center/Creator

This truth stands out in the last chapter of Joshua, which describes conditions in Canaan after the Israelites had conquered the Promised Land. Just before Joshua died, he renewed the covenant at Shechem. After recounting their history, he declared, "Now fear the LORD and serve him with all faithfulness. Throw away the gods your forefathers worshiped beyond the River and in Egypt, and serve the LORD. But if serving the LORD seems undesirable to you, then choose for yourselves this day whom you will serve. . . . But as for me and my household, we will serve the LORD" (24:14-15).

To this the people responded, "We will serve the LORD our God and obey him" (v. 24). Thus they reaffirmed the first of the Ten Commandments: "You shall have no other gods before me" (Exod. 20:3). It's the *first word* of liberation through law, the first step to freedom, to discover the freedom of truth about God.

Just as a circle can have only one center, the (singular) heart of it, so too the universe has only one Creator, the sole Source of all that is. By worshiping one God, we necessarily refuse to worship "other gods."

Rival Gods Rejected

Though much has changed since Israel entered Canaan 3,200 years ago, the "other gods" have stayed much the same; for whenever we humans worship "other gods," they are generally of two sorts: intellectual or sensual. They satisfy either our mind's curiosity or our body's lust, our head or our groin, our desire to know or our desire to control. So we deify ideas or instincts. We revere either human energies or natural physical forces.

Intellectual Gods—Baal's Heirs

The ancient world's gods were designed to meet folks' desire to know the ultimate source of life. We're intelligent creatures, and we forever hunger to know where we come from, why we're here. These are the ultimately serious kinds of questions kids ask.

One lady's six-year-old, Peter, curious concerning his origins, asked such a question: "Mom, when you get married, does that make you pregnant?"

"No," his mom answered. "Getting married is not what makes you pregnant."

"Well," he persisted, "how do you get pregnant then?"

Not wishing to get into such a serious discourse just before dinner, she answered, "Peter, it's sort of a long story."

With an impish look on his face, he cocked his head and replied, "You don't know, do you?"

Certainly there's lots about life we don't understand, but we'd like to know such things as who or what put us here. In ancient Egypt the sun god, Amon-Re, was considered the creative power shaping and sustaining all that is. In Canaan people worshiped Baal, conceived as the mysterious life force taking form in ripening wheat, grapes, olives. They understood that life comes to us from a mysterious source, an impersonal force, and they worshiped their *idea*, their explanation of nature.

Today few folks consciously worship statues such as Amon-Re and Baal. They just resurrect, rename, and worship the same ideas. For whenever we believe that an unintelligent, purposeless, natural force created the world, we in fact worship old Amon-Re or Baal. Whenever an unin-

telligent, purposeless, natural force (such as naturalistic
evolution, proceeding solely by random toss-the-dice-style
natural selection) usurps an intelligent, purposeful, supernatural Person, you find worshipers violating the first
commandment.

For over a century philosophical Darwinism has chal-
lenged the theological creationism espoused by traditional
Christianity. Many in the scientific community have, generally speaking, embraced Darwin's general notion of species
randomly evolving through natural selection—though maverick biologists from Louis Agassiz onward have questioned
and rejected its assumptions and assertions.

Recently, in *Darwin on Trial*,[1] Philip Johnson evaluated
a century of Darwinian thought and found it largely un-
persuasive. A graduate of Harvard University and the University of Chicago, Johnson clerked for Chief Justice Earl
Warren and has taught for 20 years at the University of
California at Berkeley—hardly a hotbed for fundamentalism or a haven for anti-intellectualism!

Johnson is a legal scholar accustomed to "analyzing
the logic of arguments and identifying the assumptions
that lie behind" them. He thinks himself uniquely quali-
fied to evaluate Darwinism, "because what people believe
about evolution and Darwinism depends very heavily on
the kind of logic they employ and the kind of assumptions
they make."[2] So he questions "whether Darwinism is based
upon a fair assessment of the scientific evidence, or
whether it is another kind of fundamentalism."[3] He found
it fascinating "that the very persons who insist upon keeping religion and science separate are eager to use their science as a basis for pronouncements about religion."[4]

In *The Blind Watchmaker*, for example, one of the
world's leading Darwinians, Richard Dawkins, testifies:
"Darwin made it possible to be an intellectually fulfilled
atheist."[5] Often inspired more by a spiritual longing to find

personal fulfillment than by a rigorous concern for truthful evidence, Darwinists routinely make antitheistic judgments, asserting the universe lacks design or purpose. Then they zealously evangelize, seeking (through legal coercion if necessary) converts to their views, for "mixing religion with science is obnoxious to Darwinists only when it is the wrong religion that is being mixed."[6] So long as Baal's revered, all's well!

Doctrinaire Darwinists insist "God had nothing to do with evolution," for their theory demands that everything evolves through purely natural, aimlessly random selection.[7] Maintaining and reinforcing such a naturalistic worldview, not developing a purely empirical understanding of nature, undergirds devout Darwinists' agenda, for, as they at times confess, "Evolution is, in short, the God we must worship."[8]

That the god evolution is widely worshiped stands clear to any discerning student of modernity. Consider the admission of one of the world's preeminent biologists, a 1967 Nobel peace prize winner, George Wald, who said that there are only two possible explanations for the existence of life on earth: "Creation or spontaneous generation (evolution). There is no third way. Spontaneous generation was disproved 100 years ago, but that leads us only to one other conclusion: that of supernatural creation. We cannot accept that on philosophical grounds (personal reasons); therefore, we choose to believe the impossible: that life arose spontaneously by chance."[9]

Perhaps Wald and others can, in fact, "choose to believe the impossible" and find intellectual peace; but to such worshipers the Bible declares, "You shall have no other gods before me."

Sensual Gods—Erotic Baals

In addition to intellectual gods, we easily worship gods who satisfy our lusts, especially our desire to control things. In ancient Egypt there was Isis, the fertility goddess; in ancient Canaan there were many "baals," subordinate to the high god Baal, who were usually worshiped through fertility rituals and sexual frenzies. Temple prostitutes and religious orgies pervaded the paganism of antiquity.

In some societies young women first experienced sexual intercourse as temple prostitutes; in others women had to regularly take their turn, servicing devotees of the gods. The sexual couplings were tied to the worship of a fertility goddess, or goddesses, allegedly celebrating the power of growing things, a link with the ultimate source of life.

Certainly the ancient deification of the sex goddess has revived and gained advocates in modern societies. Sigmund Freud reduced the mystery of personality to sexuality, and his more radical disciples, such as Wilhelm Reich, urged followers to find life's meaning by casting aside inhibitions and discovering the "joy of sex." Bumper stickers urge us to "do it" in various places with various persons. Films provide cultic rituals for the sexual creed. We even have temples, striptease joints, dotting the alleys and access roads of urban America, apparently attracting droves of devotees on a daily basis.

What's amazing about the deification of sex is this: Whenever sex becomes preeminent, women are exploited and sex is sterilized. Ancient temple prostitutes were *used*, so there was no concern for the ultimate purpose and normal consequence of sexual intercourse: children. The same holds today. The sexual revolution has exploited rather than liberated women. Abortion, contraception, no-fault divorce laws, and living together cohabitation all sever sexual pleasure from procreation. While some (usually young) women flaunt their newfound "freedom" to engage in various pleasures, the sexual revolution has mainly freed men to live irresponsibly.

Survey results in *The Day America Told the Truth* indicate that "in terms of the idealized couple of the past—virgins joined in holy matrimony, faithful till death them part—we found nothing but a shadow on the wall." If folks actually told the truth in this study—though other polls suggest we are less lascivious—"Ninety-two percent of sexually active people report having had ten or more lovers, with a lifetime average of seventeen. Four in ten among us have had more than one lover in the past year."[10] Yet, amazingly enough, the very people who claim to be "doing it" are finding it increasingly dissatisfying. Today's men and women both claimed "they wished they spent more time making love—but not with their current lover."[11] That's because, of course, they're in love with sex, with their sexual pleasures, rather than their lovers.

There's a fascinating book illustrating the escalating moral relativism in our society titled *Degenerate Moderns: Modernity as Rationalized Sexual Misbehavior,* by E. Michael Jones.[12] Central to Jones's argument is this thesis: "There are only two alternatives in the intellectual life: either one conforms desire to the truth or one conforms truth to desire."[13]

Since our sexual desire is enormously powerful, we all too often rationalize our sexual behavior rather than restrain it to live right. Though sexual sin in itself does great harm, the "most insidious corruption" weakening our species is "the corruption of the mind" that accompanies the rationalizing process. "One moves all too easily from sexual sins, which are probably the most common to mankind, to intellectual sins, which are the most pernicious."[14] We construct idols that sanctify our desires. That process, demonstrably evident in some of this century's most influential intellectuals, leads Jones to declare that "the verdict is clear: modernity is rationalized lust."[15]

That verdict is confirmed by the study of recent, frequently muckraking biographies. We now know formerly hidden details about the men and women whose theories have so shaped modernity. Consider first the case of Margaret Mead, for decades one of the most trusted and widely quoted academic anthropologists, whose *Coming of Age in Samoa* has been routinely cited as evidence for "cultural relativism." What's right in one culture, she argued, celebrating the Samoans' sexual permissiveness, may be judged wrong in another. But nothing is really right or wrong except as one responds to his or her situation.

Recent evaluations of Mead's studies, a careful checking of her sources and data, have raised a barrage of flak (items of fact) that threaten to shatter her renown. Amazingly, Mead spent only nine months in Samoa, taking a scant six weeks to "learn" the language of the people. Yet she claimed to write a "definitive" scholarly study with such superficial study! What she seems to have done, in fact, was to project her own sexual fantasies and standards onto a people she scarcely understood.

In fact, rather than being sexually libertine, the Samoans were actually a bit old-fashioned, valuing such things as virginity. Mead claimed adultery caused no stir in Samoan society, when in fact it was punishable by death. Determined to prove her teacher Franz Boas's doctrine of cultural relativism, she cavalierly imposed on the Samoans what she imagined primitive peoples, untainted by civilized moral standards, would live out. Herself involved in an adulterous affair, "Mead's guilty imagination projected adultery onto the puritanical Samoans."[16]

Psychoanalysis, founded by Sigmund Freud and Carl Jung, stamps modernity like a trademark. Jones devotes his longest chapter to these two, arguing that Jung's 40-year adulterous relationship with Toni Wolff and Freud's allegedly incestuous affair clearly helped shape their sexually permissive, rationalizing psychologies. Carefully examined, some of Freud's most significant theories—the Oedipus complex, totemism, primitive sexual promiscuity—have absolutely no basis in historical or anthropological fact. Actually, "The oldest and ethnologically most primitive people . . . know nothing whatsoever of totemism, and in fact their religion has striking similarities to both Judaism and Christianity in that these people tend to be monotheistic and monogamous, and even refer to God as 'Our Father.'"[17]

When we consider the gods of antiquity, comparing them with those of modernity, it's clear some things persist throughout human history. There's something latent within human nature that leads us to look for gods who validate our desires. We deify ideas or instincts. We construct sophisticated ideas to explain natural processes, call them Baal or evolution, and follow their constructs. Or we elevate elemental instincts, especially our sexual desires, and call them baals or "madonnas" or porn magazines or promiscuous film "stars" and obey their edicts and examples.

In truth, we're "gonna have to serve somebody"! Or, as Joshua said, "Choose for yourselves this day whom you will serve"!

NEW TESTAMENT INTERNALIZATION: SERVE GOD

Turning to the New Testament, we see that the first commandment gains a Christian imperative in the call to discipleship. In responding to the call of Jesus, we find a singular commitment to service, an exclusive allegiance to Him, which makes more personal and intimate the command to put God first in our lives. In the Christian life, as in other realms of reality, priorities establish the quality of existence.

John Wooden, the University of California, Los Angeles (UCLA) great basketball coach, perhaps the greatest ever to coach college basketball, begins his autobiography, *They Call Me Coach*, with a short poem by George Moriarty:

Who can ask more of a man
than giving all within his span?
Giving all, it seems to me,
is not so far from victory.[18]

Wooden insists that as a coach he rarely talked about winning. What he stressed was giving one's all. And if you can get five well-coached, physically talented basketball players to give their all, you do in fact win a lot of games. The secret to success is commitment to excellence.

What's true on the basketball court is also true in the physics lab. "The laws of physics should be simple," said Albert Einstein in a lecture.

"But what if they are not simple?" someone asked.

Said Einstein, "Then I would not be interested in them."[19] Einstein wanted to comprehend the cosmos, to read the mind of God, so he couldn't clutter his mind with trivial data.

To play basketball well, to do physics well, to live well, to love well—whatever we do well—demands singular commitment. It demands our all. It's all or nothing at all! Still more: to follow Jesus calls for nothing less than our *all*. When C. S. Lewis found himself captivated by God, he also sensed that "total surrender, the absolute leap in the dark, were demanded. The reality with which no treaty can be made was upon me. The demand was not even 'All or nothing.' . . . Now, the demand was simply 'All.'"[20]

So Jesus' words in Luke 9:57-62 illuminate the *allness* of the great commandment, which is that we are to love the Lord our God with all our heart, soul, mind, and strength. In the New Testament the old covenant, including the Ten Commandments, is fulfilled as the law of the Lord is internalized and amplified in the lives of Jesus' followers. For if we *love* God rightly, we'll have no problems with "other gods." Luke's Gospel says, "As they were walking along the road, a man said to him, 'I will follow you wherever you go.' Jesus replied, 'Foxes have holes and birds of the air have nests, but the Son of Man has no place to lay his head'" (9:57-58).

Tune Out! Toss Off the Tyranny of Pleasure

This "wanna-be" disciple feared discomfort. Human beings, in general, allow the "pleasure principle" to reign like a dictator over them. The prospective disciple illustrates this. He rather liked what he saw in Jesus, thinking it might be nice to tag along. But Jesus sensed the man's commitment to comfort. We, like him, too regularly choose comfort, ignoring its hidden costs, "letting it all hang out." If it feels good, we do it. We're like Oscar Wilde, who said, "I can resist anything but temptation."[21] We choose the easy way—though we know the path of least resistance makes persons as crooked as mountain streams.

While visiting my brother and sister-in-law in Kansas City, I was awakened one morning by my nephew's voice. "Mom . . . Mom . . . Mom." His mother was drying her hair and couldn't hear him. But he continued: "Mom . . . Mom." In time his dad went to him. They talked briefly, and then I heard Larry say: "Now, Toby, you can pull up the covers yourself—you don't need Mom to do it for you." The lazy little rascal wouldn't even pull up his own covers when he felt cold! He wanted Mom to do it!

There's a story about a little guy, aged seven, who informed his mother at breakfast that he had decided to drop out of school. She asked why, and he said, "Because it's too hard, it's too long, and it's too boring." In response, his mom looked long and hard into his eyes and said, "Johnny, you've just described *life!* Get your coat on, get out the door, and get on that bus!"

It's easy to do the easy thing. We excuse that in children. It's easy to get addicted to pleasure—there are millions of pleasure addicts as well as alcoholics and drug addicts. It's easier to sleep in rather than go to class, church, or work.

(I just urge my students to get up and go. If you fall asleep somewhere, at least you may get credit for being there.)

It's easier to eat another dip of ice cream than another helping of broccoli. It's easier to drive your car than to walk a block. We're basically lazy, and we easily choose the easy way. We're comfort addicts! But Jesus calls us to the straight and narrow way that leads to life everlasting. If we want to be His disciples, we need to find Robert Frost's "road . . . less traveled," the oft uncomfortable way of the Son of God, who had no place to lay His head.

Turn In! Now Is Our Hour! Stop Procrastinating!

Returning to our biblical story, Jesus "said to another man, 'Follow me.' But the man replied, 'Lord, first let me go and bury my father.' Jesus said to him, 'Let the dead bury their own dead, but you go and proclaim the kingdom of God" (Luke 9:59-60).

The second wanna-be disciple talked things over with Jesus and wanted to go home and bury his father. In the Semitic world this expression meant the son wanted to stay at home until his father died—which could be another 40 years! Jesus' response had nothing to do with attending a scheduled funeral. The inquirer apparently wanted to live securely under his father's protection, gaining the security that would come through inheriting his father's property, and then think about following Jesus. He represents the attitude of day-by-day delay.

Too often we waste away our lives. Day by day we expend our energies building sand castles, buying plastic jewelry that quickly collects in cardboard boxes. We flush our lives down the tube—the television tube. Television, something we should control, too often controls us. We become "couch potatoes" with our seats stuck to La-Z-Boys and our eyes glued to the colored tube.

Comedian Fred Allen supposedly said, "Television is a device that permits people who haven't anything to do to watch people who can't do anything." Still more, he suspected that the reason TV is called a "medium" is that rarely is anything on it well done![22]

I think the great threat of TV is not its evil content—though there's room for concern there. The great threat of TV is its mesmerizing ability to detach us from reality, to fixate us in fantasies, so that we literally waste away our lives. To us—to all of us immersed in videoland—Jesus says urgently: "Don't waste your life!" For now is our hour.

In the opinion of Neil Postman, an educator, television has become our era's *truly subversive*, mind-molding medium. It's today's lingua franca. Thus he argues, in *Amusing Ourselves to Death*,[23] that the electronic media, particularly television, have degraded American culture. Speaking as plainly as possible, Postman analyzes and laments what he judges "the most significant American cultural fact" of our times, "the ascendancy of the Age of Television." This development absolutely alters every aspect of life, demanding that "politics, religion, education, and anything else that comprises public business" conform, like athletic contests breaking for commercials, to TV's dicta.[24]

TV's triumph consummates what began a century ago, when the print-based culture, thriving on reflective thought and exposition, began caving in to "the Age of Show Business," wherein electronic-powered media (e.g., telegraphed news and photographed pictures) shifted folks' attention from substance to style, from the realities embedded in firsthand experiences to images and illusions transported from afar.[25] In the process, an addictive drug, entertainment, unleashed its demands that politics, education, and religion be packaged in visually attractive ways. The image became more important, more than preeminent, and it effectively *displaced* reality.

We're called to live in our day, to avoid putting off until tomorrow what we can do today. The world's not standing still. Nor can we! When we come to the end of our days, I wonder how we'll evaluate the time we spent watching TV, the hours invested in attending spectator sports events and concerts. Do we want to be remembered as people who wanted to be entertained? I sometimes wonder what message will be on my tombstone. How sad it would be to have it chiseled in stone that "He never missed an NFL game," or "She always watched Oprah."

Take Off! Cast Off the Paralysis of the Past

The third wanna-be disciple said to Jesus, "I will follow you, Lord; but first let me go back and say good-by to my family." To this Jesus replied: "No one who puts his hand to the plow and looks back is fit for service in the kingdom of God" (Luke 9:61-62).

The man in this story wanted to keep his bases covered, his options open, his security blanket in place. He wanted to go home, to keep personal ties alive, to preserve a network of personal contacts. He wanted to follow Jesus—but he also wanted to make sure his "significant others" weren't alienated. He feared to break with his past, to distance himself from his comfortable kinsfolk. He allowed the past to dictate the present. Like him, we are often tempted to allow old relationships, ingrained habits, toughened ties to what has happened to us, to dictate our future.

Rather than wasting our lives, being entertained to death, Jesus calls us to new ventures, to adventures, to breakthroughs into the unknown. We need to live in the only time allotted us to live—in the now. If we live well, we'll learn to take the *firsts*, not the *bests*, as they come. Generally speaking, we need to take the first opportunity rather than waiting for the perfect situation.

When World War II broke out, Martin Gray, 14 years old, began fighting with the Jewish resistance forces in Warsaw. Twice captured by the Nazis and sent to death camps, he twice escaped. He did so because he resolved to take the *first*, not the *best*, chance. He lived while others died, because he grabbed the less-than-safe opportunities.

I've tried to learn from Martin Gray. I've found there are many things I can do if I act when I can. My wife and I decided to take trips before we're so decrepit we have to tour about in wheelchairs. I've climbed mountains—Colorado's highest peaks and Mount Whitney in California. I've run marathons. In many instances my knee (which has been a problem for 20 years) was less than perfectly sound. But I hiked and ran. I've rarely done anything when everything was perfectly right. But if it's worth doing, take the first good opportunity. Don't waste time waiting for the perfect opening.

The legendary Satchel Paige, one of the greatest pitchers in baseball history, stayed athletically active until he was (some think) nearly 60 years old. Asked the secret of his longevity, he said, "Don't look back. Something may be gaining on you."[26] Life's ahead of us, not behind us. Satchel Paige suffered race discrimination and knew the indignity of not having his true talents rightly rewarded. But throughout his life he refused to grow bitter. He did what he could with what he had. And he lived by his motto.

So too, in following Jesus there are wanna-bes and gonna-bes. If we're to be His disciples, we must do more than wanna-be. And if we do in fact follow Him, committed to being disciples, we fulfill, as New Testament believers, the first commandment: "You shall have no other gods before me" (Exod. 20:3).

4

A Sacrosanct Focus

OLD TESTAMENT FOUNDATION: NO IDOLS ALLOWED

On her way to the hospital to give birth to another baby, a mom told her little boy that she would return with a "gift from God." A couple of days later, peering into the baby crib, the little guy seriously interrogated the new baby, saying: "Quick, little brother, before you forget—what's God like?"

Lots of us would like to know! If you could describe God, what would He look like? What image of God washes around in your head? How do you understand Him and His ways? Are we trying to understand God perfectly, perhaps to reduce Him to something we can handle, something as predictable as the geometric deductions we mastered as high school sophomores learning plane geometry?

As a preacher, I often feel awkward serving as an advocate for an "invisible" God. We can't easily abide the ambiguity wrapped up in the ultimate mystery of God, the mystery expressed in one of Annie Dillard's poems:

> My sister
> dreamed of a sculpture
> showing the form of God.
> He has no edges,
> and the holes in him spin.

He alone is real,
and all things lie in him
as fossil shells
curl in solid shale.
My sister dreamed of God
who moves around
the spanding, shattered holes
of solar systems hollowed in his side.[1]

Then there's the medieval description penned by Hildovert of Lavardin, which says:

God is over all things,
under all things,
outside all;
within, but not enclosed,
without, but not excluded,
above, but not raised up,
below, but not depressed,
wholly without, embracing,
wholly within, filling.

To suggest the true infinity of God, many theologians suggest imagining God as a circle whose center is everywhere—and whose circumference is nowhere. Unfortunately, many of us tend to make ourselves God's center and our concerns His circumference! Rather than trying to be like God, we make God like us—something much easier to accomplish. Worse yet, some of us try to reduce God to nice, manageable forms, like cookie cutters, useful idols designed to make life more comfortable. Indeed, as Martin Luther said in *Table Talk,* "We easily fall into idolatry, for we are inclined thereunto by nature, and coming to us by inheritance, it seems pleasant."[2]

Substituting Means for Ends

But the second of the Ten Commandments forbids idolatry. The first commandment isolates the *Object* of our worship, the Source of our theology, insisting we have no

other gods but Yahweh. The second commandment high-
lights the *means* whereby we worship, our liturgy. Scripture tells us that to sustain a covenant relationship with
God, to live really with Him, we're not to manufacture
idols imaging earthly things. Indeed: "You shall not bow
down to them or worship them; for I, the LORD your God,
am a jealous God" (Exod. 20:5).

Religiously, we often elevate means above ends. We
want to worship God, but we become obsessed with certain ways to do so—or not to do so. We devise sophisticated strategies, often of great artistic ingenuity, whereby to
approach and serve God. Idolatry, rightly understood, simply means focusing on the means (how we worship) rather
than the End (the One we worship).

My wife, Roberta, is a fine cook. However, since moving to San Diego, where we get two-for-the-price-of-one
coupons for meals in many restaurants, she has radically
reduced her time in the kitchen. I guess she's kind of a
"kitchen dropout." One of her friends gave her a slogan at-
tached to a magnet, to be placed on the refrigerator, declaring, "Kitchen closed. Gone shopping." But when she does
cook, Roberta is a fine cook.

Just imagine, however, that she decided to demon-
strate her love for me by giving herself full-time to cooking. Day after day, all day long, she'd shop for the finest
foods in the most exclusive specialty shops. She'd prepare
unique and tasty breakfasts and dinners. Her skills as a
gourmet cook would shine like a star.

In fact, she'd make sure her talents were evident to all.
She'd invite numerous guests to join us at every meal—
making sure they knew she was giving herself completely
to cooking meals for me, showing her love for me. Further
imagine that, as time went on, she became so busy prepar-
ing and serving the food, entertaining the guests, demon-
strating her devotion, that she never sat down and ate with

me. In fact, morning, noon, and night, she would say little or nothing to me.

Should that happen, it would be obvious that my wife had become obsessed with *means*—the cooking that demonstrates her good wifely character—rather than *ends:* maintaining a warm relationship with me, her husband for whom she was cooking. In truth, the really important thing about mealtime is the fact it enables us to *be together*, to talk together, just to look at each other. If my wife reduced our relationship to *her activity*, cooking, I'd soon tire of the good food and start skipping meals—knowing she'd keep on cooking and entertaining folks because she wanted to impress the world with her devotion to me.

Similarly, we break fellowship with God when we get so obsessed with the *ways* we do things, the ways we sing or serve, that we forget *why* we're doing them, for *whom* we're doing them. When we reduce God to human scale, focusing on our ways of doing things, we become idolatrous.

Years ago Amy Grant was asked to sing in her home church in Tennessee. She was 15 years old and wanted to accompany herself with a guitar. She asked her father if she could, and he told her to ask one of the congregation's elders, for her church had traditionally allowed no musical instruments in its services. Amazingly, the elder said yes. So Amy sang, guitar resounding. As a result, some of the older people quit the church. The man who permitted Amy to sing, however, said he did so because the "no-instrument doctrine" had become an idol that needed to be broken. And Amy, he thought, was the one to break it.

If we can't worship without organ music, we've made the organ an idol. If we can't worship without guitar music, we have a guitar-shaped idol. If we can't worship except to the tune of traditional hymns, we've cast them as gold-gilded idols. If we can't worship except while singing contemporary praise choruses, we've created new idols. If

we refuse to listen to preachers unless they sound like
Chuck Swindoll or Robert Schuller, we've turned little men
into little idols.

Whenever we become fanatical about something, fab-
ricating an ism of some sort, we turn idolatrous. "A fanatic," wrote Finley Peter Dunne ("Mr. Dooley"), "is a man
who does what he thinks th' Lord wud do if he knew th'
facts iv th' case."[3]

Whenever we brand "absolute" our own parochial
"truths" and goals, we turn fanatical. The word "fanatic"
comes from a Latin word *fanum,* meaning "temple." It
means "unreasonably enthusiastic; overly zealous; unduly
devoted to some cause." Sports fans idolize athletes and
teams; music fans idolize musicians and songs; academic
fans idolize prestigious professors and theories. Religious
fans idolize charismatic preachers and peculiar theologies.
We can even idolize spiritual ideals, truths, and goods of
various sorts that we love more than God.

Importantly, fanatics forever weave of their dreams a
utopian paradise. Oblivious to reality, they incessantly talk
about how things *ought* to be. Indeed, they excel in chart-
ing how the world *will* be in the future. Utopians overflow
with visions of some heaven on earth. And the paradise is
always for a small sect, usually composed of the dreamer
and his or her friends.

In 1836 Thomas Arnold wrote a letter to A. P. Stanley,
thoughtfully exploring this issue:

Fanaticism is idolatry; and it has the moral evil of
idolatry in it; that is, a fanatic worships something which
is the creation of his own desire, and thus even his self-
devotion in support of it is only an apparent self-devo-
tion; for in fact it is making the parts of his nature or his
mind, which he least values, offer sacrifice to that which
he most values. The moral fault, as it appears to me, is
the idolatry—the setting up of some idea which is most
kindred to our own minds, and the putting it in the place

of Christ, who alone cannot be made an idol and inspire idolatry, because He combines all ideas of perfection and exhibits them in their just harmony and combination.[4]

Substituting Things for a Person

We also make idols when we revere things rather than a divine Person, when we prefer gifts to the Giver, when we use persons so as to enjoy things rather than using things so as to enjoy persons.

Imagine another scenario. Imagine that years ago I had started bringing home a present for my wife each time I returned from a trip. Since I travel quite a bit, the gifts would begin to add up. Imagine that my wife *expected* me to bring her a gift *every* time I came home—and that it was evident that she wanted a *nicer* gift each time. If I failed to bring a present, she would not talk with me for a week. If the gift was a bit "cheap," she would sulk and complain that I really didn't love her very much.

It would become clear that she spent most of her time caring for the collection of gifts: polishing them, putting them in fine display cases, talking about them with her friends, talking with me only when things were at issue. One day, as you would suspect, it would dawn on me that she cared for me only as a *supplier* of gifts. She really liked the stuff I bought her, not the person who brought them to her. In treasuring the things more than the person who brought them, she would fray the marriage bond, the loving commitment between two persons.

Now God created the material world, so material things help us understand some things about Him. Many things serve as useful analogies. An anonymous analogist recently compiled a list of analogies, suggesting,

> *God is like Coca-Cola . . .*
> *He's the real thing.*
> *God is like Bayer aspirin . . .*
> *He works wonders.*

> *God is like Hallmark cards . . .*
>   *He cares enough to send the very best.*
> *God is like VO5 hair spray . . .*
>   *He works through all kinds of weather.*
> *God is like Dial soap . . .*
>   *Aren't you glad you know Him?*
> *God is like Scotch tape . . .*
>   *You can't see Him, but you know He's there.*
> *God is like American Express . . .*
>   *Don't leave home without Him.*

Such analogies are fine, even helpful, if we remember they are simply ways of imagining, as long as we remember the Person they point to. In my opinion, the only way we can think at all about God is analogically. Material things, physical symbols, artistic works effectively direct our attention to nonmaterial, nonphysical realities.

If you consider the list of analogies above, some of them are enlightening. Sure enough, God's the real thing! So He's sort of like Coca-Cola. But if you treat Coca-Cola as the real thing, reverently drinking the magical fluid in hopes of life everlasting, you have turned an analogy into an idol.

Clearly God, like Bayer aspirin, has worked and still works wonders. But if you decide that God's a great chunk of aspirin, that He functions only to alleviate your pain, and you reverently pop pills in order to cope with life, you're idolatrous. It's true that God works through all kinds of weather. But if you decide God's a great big bottle of VO5, interested in nothing else except helping you look nice, you've reduced Him to an object, ever anxious to serve you. It's true that God's invisible, like Scotch tape. But if you decide God's just a bundle of sticky tape, anxious to patch up the messes you make, you've shaped an idol, an image of God in your own likeness. Yes, God's like an American Express card—and you shouldn't leave home without Him. But if you decide God's an unlimited credit card—far better than gold, or platinum, sort of a "Diamond Divine" card, eternally covering all our expenses—you turn idolatrous.

The Book of Numbers tells how the Israelites in the wilderness grumbled about the food (manna), wanting God to give them more palatable stuff. They complained so much that God sent poisonous snakes among them. While some folks were dying, others grew repentant and asked Moses to pray for them. In response to Moses' prayer, "The LORD said to Moses, 'Make a snake and put it up on a pole; anyone who is bitten can look at it and live'" (21:8). This Moses did, and the snake became a symbol of God's mercy. So long as it remained a symbol, reminding people of God, it was a blessed memento. It was an *icon*, a holy symbol.

Seven centuries later, however, the snake became an *idol*. The people of Israel began worshiping the symbol, not the God whose mercy it represented. So King Hezekiah, when he reformed the nation, "broke into pieces the bronze snake Moses had made" (2 Kings 18:4). A marvelous sign of deliverance had been twisted into an idolatrous talisman, a thing of magic and power before which folks burned incense and worshiped.

For idolatry essentially is power worship, often employing magical means. When we turn to things we've made, seeking power from them, we worship idols. When we believe the good life consists in the accumulation of goods, we've made idols. When we actually embrace maxims such as "Better living through chemistry," we turn idolatrous.

Though we're tempted to isolate idolatry to ancient eras, in fact we live in a thoroughly idolatrous culture. Our industrial society, stamping out goods with cookie-cutter efficiency, sets before us an almost infinite number of idols that give or promise to give us infinite power. In the words of Joy Davidman:

Idolatry lies not in the idol but in the worshiper. It is a psychological attitude that governs his whole life, and a very murderous attitude. We begin by offering others to the idol; we end by offering ourselves. Men threw their babies into the fiery furnace of Molech and threw themselves before the crushing car of Jagannath; men unconsciously sacrifice themselves and their children daily to the automobile juggernaut and the brain-consuming furnace of the modern city.[5]

Somewhat similarly, the great Nicaraguan poet Ernesto Cardinal wrote:

Modern materialism is not very different from ancient polytheism, and the world has never worshipped as many idols as today. Cars, movie stars, political leaders, ideologies are the modern idols—the idols of commercial advertising and the idols of political propaganda, the smiling goddesses of fertility and material abundance, quack medicines and hygiene, the gods of beer, corn flakes and dentifrices; the faces of dictators and political bosses and the somber deities of terror and war, of destruction and death.[6]

Yet the Word of God stands: "You shall not make for yourself a graven image. . . . you shall not bow down to them or serve them" (Exod. 20:4-5, RSV). So if you're tempted to reduce God to cookie cutters, useful and usable for you—the magic door to the goods of the good life—think again!

NEW TESTAMENT INTERNALIZATION: WHAT'S REALLY LIVING?

Several years ago Tony Campolo told about a man who asked

to be buried seated behind the wheel of a brand-new Cadillac, dressed in a tuxedo, with a two-dollar cigar in his mouth. He left the money to insure that his wish would be fulfilled, and it was. The undertaker brought in a huge crane to maneuver the automobile-casket for the dead man. As he pulled the handle lowering the corpse and Cadillac into the ground, the crane operator was heard to say, "Man—that's really living!"[7]

I wonder what we consider "really living." If you're a go-getter, what is it, do you suppose, you'll get in the end? To some, according to a modern T-shirt, "He who dies with the most toys wins." Or, as I saw on a San Diego license plate-holder: "She who dies with the most clothes wins." In the end, we're told, what really counts is only what we can count! Historian L. S. Stavrianos declares that many, if not all of us, say: "What is the chief end of man?—to get rich. In what way?—dishonestly if we can; honestly if we must. Who is God, the only one and true? Money is god."[8]

There's an addiction worse than alcoholism. There's a disease worse than AIDS. It's the idolatry of money, the voracious lust for money that sacrifices everything for monetary gain. In the Sermon on the Mount Jesus addressed this very issue, deepening the dimensions of the second commandment, which insisted we discard idols and worship God alone. In William Barclay's judgment, "Surely there is no better description of a man's god than to say that his god is the power in whom he trusts; and when a man puts his trust in material things, then material things have become, not his support, but his god."[9]

In Matthew's Gospel, seeking to focus our faith on God alone, Jesus calls us to the freedom of serving the Liberator Creator rather than idols of our own creation:

> Do not store up for yourselves treasures on earth, where moth and rust destroy, and where thieves break in and steal. But store up for yourselves treasures in heaven, where moth and rust do not destroy, and where thieves do not break in and steal. For where your treasure is, there your heart will be also.
> The eye is the lamp of the body. If your eyes are good, your whole body will be full of light. But if your

eyes are bad, your whole body will be full of darkness. If then the light within you is darkness, how great is that darkness!

No one can serve two masters. Either he will hate the one and love the other, or he will be devoted to the one and despise the other. You cannot serve both God and Money *(6:19-24).*

The word translated "Money" was an Aramaic word, *mamon,* which meant material possessions. In our society it best represents a collage of "things, money, gain, or success."[10] For us, mammon means "Making It."[11] At issue, of course, is not *having* such goods, but *serving* them. As Martin Luther said: "The emphasis here is on the little word 'serve.' It is no sin to have money and property, wife and children, house and home. But you must not let it be your master. You must make it serve you, and you must be its master."[12]

Jesus talked frequently about money. Sixteen of His 38 parables dealt with it; one out of every 10 verses in the Gospels refers to it. Though major themes, such as prayer and faith, are mentioned in 500 verses, money appears in 2,000! Clearly it was a big issue to Jesus. That's because it's so easy to serve money rather than God. Indeed, it's easy to make money our god. In our quest for happiness we're tempted to think hoarding money enables us to attain it. As Arthur Schopenhauer said, "Money is human happiness in the abstract: he, then, who is no longer capable of enjoying human happiness in the concrete devotes himself utterly to money."[13]

It's Easy to Worship/Serve Money

So we must understand that, as Jacques Ellul writes, "what Jesus is revealing is that money is power."[14] The world's movers and shakers, our heroes, must earn millions, for we equate success with income. They've "made it," we think. We know that some of them, like Janis Joplin, now and then lament, "Now that I'm here, where am I?" But the rest of us still push on, assuming we'll feel differently when we reach the top.

We also hope as a society to prosper, to see an ever increasing standard of living. Presidents, as George Bush discovered, are summarily retired if the nation's economy sags a bit! In 1930 John Maynard Keynes, one of the most influential economists of this century, the main architect of the deficit-spending welfare state that is so prevalent, looked forward to the day when everyone would prosper and have the comfort necessary to enable us "once more to value needs above means and prefer the good to the useful."[15]

However, Keynes declared, "Beware! The time for all this is not yet. For at least another hundred years we must pretend to ourselves that fair is foul and foul is fair; for foul is useful and fair is not. Avarice and usury and precaution must be our gods for a little longer still. For only they can lead us out of the tunnel of economic necessity into daylight."[16]

In *The Day America Told the Truth*, folks responded to the question "What are you willing to do for $10 million?" Some 25 percent of the respondents would abandon their families or their churches; 23 percent would turn prostitutes for a week or more; 16 percent would give up their United States citizenship; 7 percent would kill an innocent stranger.[17] Recently 3,000 women responded to a Virginia Slims opinion poll that asked what would make their lives better. Three percent marked "a better sex life." Eight percent wanted "a different relationship." But 60 percent (more than twice the percentage of the second-place item) said, "More money." Some little girls, barely into grammar school, were asked to state their fondest wish. They could think of nothing grander than to have $5 million—and two days in a mall![18] We do, as people, *love* money. And we're apparently willing to *serve* it in various ways.

It's Essential That We Worship/Serve God Alone

Now Jesus, God's Son, dares us to reject the very thing our culture most admires—money. He wants us to see the realities of life. Money and success are abstractions, not realities. They're idolatrous images that we worship and pursue. But they never truly satisfy, for they elude finality. In fact, they effectively enslave and ultimately damn us. Jacques Ellul says: "When we claim to use money, we make a gross error. We can, if we must, use money, but it is really money that uses us and makes us servants by bringing us under its law and subordinating us to its aims."[19]

When we fall under mammon's spell, we go astray in life. Noted Harvard economist John Kenneth Galbraith concluded: "The pursuit of money, or any enduring association with it, is capable of inducing not only bizarre but ripely perverse behavior."[20] Consider the bizarre and perverse behavior that erupted in 1930 when Henrietta Garrett died at the age of 81. She left $17 million in her estate and no will. One cousin survived, as did half a dozen friends. Yet in time 26,000 persons from 29 different countries, hiring 3,000 lawyers, tried to prove they were Mrs. Garrett's legal heirs!

In the process they perjured themselves in court, fabricated family records, legally changed their names, falsified records in church Bibles, and made up improbable tales of illegitimacy. Consequently, 12 were fined, 10 went to jail, 2 committed suicide, and 3 were murdered.[21] Idolatry exacts its price!

The Generosity Key

Rich men frequently find no joy in wealth, not because of the wealth itself, but because, as Jesus said, their eyes are darkened. Their riches, like cataracts, dim their vision. They need enlightened eyes—good eyes.

The word often translated "single" in this text (KJV) is better translated "generous." Good eyes are generous eyes.

Bad eyes (*ponēros* in the Greek) means "niggardly, grudg-
ing and ungenerous."[22] A good eye, a generous eye, sees
money as something to use for good, not something to
hoard as if it were in itself good.

When the Emperor Decius (ca. A.D. 250) was persecut-
ing the Church, some of his emissaries barged into a
church and demanded that its deacon, Laurentius, give
them the treasures they had heard were buried therein. In
response, Laurentius pointed out the sick who were being
attended, the widows and orphans getting food, and said,
"These are the treasures of the Church."[23] At its best the
Church and its faithful testify to the truth that "it is more
blessed to give than to receive" (Acts 20:35), to have a good
eye, looking for opportunity to share God's gifts.

Both windows and mirrors are made of glass. Mirrors
are nice when you're getting ready to face the world in the
morning. I much prefer shaving with a mirror to guide my
razor. But I don't want to live in a house of mirrors. I want
windows to open up my awareness of my world. To live in
a windowless house would be intolerable to me. To live in
a house with mirrors instead of windows would prove utterly oppressive. The only difference between the glass that
enables me to see out, to see the world, and the mirror that
reflects myself is a thin layer of silver behind the glass,
which makes the mirror a mirror.

That's what money does. It coats the windows of our
hearts and minds with silver, keeping us from seeing as we
ought to see, keeping us from living as we ought to live—
open to and aware of the world of God and man around us.

5

A Hallowed Name Above All Names

OLD TESTAMENT FOUNDATION: TAKE NOT GOD'S NAME IN VAIN

The Bible reveals a God who *presents* himself to us, calling us to enter into a loving relationship, a *covenant*, with Him. He has specified in the Ten Commandments proper ways to do so: 10 steps to freely maintain fellowship with Him. The third commandment says, "You shall not take the name of the LORD your God in vain" (Exod. 20:7, NASB). It could be translated, "You shall not misuse or abuse the name of Yahweh," or "You shall not frivolously name God's name." To walk with God, we clearly must know and revere His name, for names really matter!

Relationships occur and endure only among people who know each other by name. Anonymous relationships exist no more than love between strangers passing in the night. Loving bonds stay knit when people revere each other's names. And the most precious relationship available to us, made possible by the God who is really present with us, demands that we take not "the name of the LORD your God in vain."

Years ago I was ordained as a minister. In our denomination, ordination services climax a district assembly and are notably solemn events, invested with sacred language and liturgy. My wife and I were kneeling, along with other ordinands, at the altar. The general superintendent came to me, placed his hand on my head, read some liturgical phrases, and intoned, "Gerald Reed, I ordain . . ." At that point the sacredness of the moment dissolved for my wife and me. We were instantly amused rather than blessed. The ordination, strangely enough, seemed irrelevant to me—for my name is *Gerard*, not Gerald!

I like my name. My name and I are integrally united. I've always liked my name and strongly resisted efforts to reduce it to nicknames such as "Jerry." Telephone solicitors who call and warmly purr, "Hello—is this Gerald?" are coolly informed that "This is *Gerard* speaking!" Much of my life has been invested in correcting documents and introductions that label me "Gerald."

Gerard is a French name that means "bright, shining spear," a rather militant label. It's akin to Gerhard in German, Gerardo in Spanish. My parents selected the name because they listened to a radio program that was popular in the early 1940s, *The Quiz Kids*. They liked a smart little guy named Gerard and named me for him. Whether or not I've lived up to my namesake, I like my name. Somehow it's important to me.

So if you want to initiate and cultivate a relationship with me, don't call me "Gerald" or "Jerry"! Names really matter. As a teacher, I try to learn my students' names. For there's a mystical warmth generated when people remember names. And relationships survive by revering the sacredness of names. So the Bible tells us to be careful when we use God's name.

Perjury Proscribed

Most clearly, the third commandment refers to using God's name to sanctify a lie. When a person is called into court as a witness and swears on a Bible "to tell the truth, the whole truth, and nothing but the truth, so help me

God," he or she assumes a sacred obligation. To commit perjury, to lie under oath, is the most obvious violation of the third commandment. As Philo wrote, "To invoke God to attest the truth of a lie is a most impious deed."[1]

Now I've never been called as a witness in a court trial. I doubt I ever will. Maybe I'm just not hanging around the right crowd! But this commandment still applies to me, for I've made some very *public* vows, calling upon God as my witness, vows that I'm honor-bound to keep. When I was baptized, at the age of 12, it was "in the name of the Father and of the Son and of the Holy Spirit." Taking the name of the Holy Trinity, I vowed to turn from sin and live for God.

Ten years later I stood before an altar, in the presence of God and a great company of witnesses, and promised to be faithful to my wife for the rest of my life. Were I to walk away from her, I'd be walking away from God as well, for in breaking my marriage vow, I'd be taking God's name in vain as well. Solemn vows, invoking God's name, demand we uphold the promises we've made.

Profanity Prohibited

More than perjury, profanity is also prohibited. When we profane something, we degrade what is good. Profane language degrades good words, reducing them to rubbish. The word "profane" comes from two Latin words: *pro,* meaning before, and *fanum,* meaning temple. To profane means to drag out holy things from the temple, to degrade them. Profanely using God's name reduces to filth the most lofty, sacred name in our language.

I wish I could say this commandment prohibits vulgar or dirty language, because I don't like dirty mouths any more than I like dirty faces or feet. I appreciate No Smoking sections in restaurants, and I would even more endorse No Swearing sections in public places. If TV advertisements are right, the slightest hint of bad breath or body odor alienates those who might find you attractive. So one would assume that a filthy mouth drives even wider wedges between those who have a healthy sensitivity to verbal pollution and those who do not.

Clearly, as a cover story in *Time* magazine indicates, we're immersed in "Dirty Words—America's Foul-Mouthed Pop Culture."[2] If we have ears, and most of us clearly do, we know how much filth washes about our verbal atmosphere. Perhaps we've decided, along with Mark Twain, to "swear while we may, for in heaven it will not be allowed."[3]

Though I think we need to watch our language, to be as averse to filthy speech as to body odor, that's admittedly more my own conviction than the meaning of the third commandment. For the profanity that's forbidden is the language that robs God's name of the sanctity due it. Joy Davidman rightly insists that this commandment "is not just a nice-Nellyish warning against profanity. It is much more like the sort of warning you see around power plants: 'Danger—High Voltage!' For the ancient Hebrews seem to have thought of God almost literally as a live wire."[4]

Truly, some things are too sacred to be profaned. We all understand and follow that truth. And some words have become taboo. If you're a TV newscaster, you don't use the word "nigger"—there would be protests and lawsuits if you did. If Dan Rather started calling gay men "queers," ACT-UP and other pressure groups would demand his removal. On some university campuses, official publications ban "incorrect" speech, language that is sexually or racially off limits. Words must be watched, monitored, to avoid offending some folks.

Students at Ivy League universities have been punished for making racially insensitive remarks. A distinguished professor had to quit teaching a class because he failed in his lectures to conform to some of his students' stereotypes of Native Americans. Among other things, he used the word "Indian" (which is currently forbidden in voguishly liberal circles, though many *real* Navajo and Sioux cheerfully continue to use it). We are, in fact, concerned about words. The language we use, what we say about certain persons or groups of persons, matters.

Yet you can, without social disapproval—much less legal penalty—profanely use God's name! Public figures who would never insult African-Americans by using the word "nigger" routinely profane God's name. But Scripture speaks clearly: we're not to take God's name in vain by cursing. David Seamands saw a bit of graffiti in a rest room that declared: "'Damn' is not God's last name."[5] How true!

There is, of course, a strangely religious dimension to swearing. Folks who swear—even atheists who swear—indirectly invoke God. When they are angry, they might use God's name in vain, not Bill Clinton's. When they've smashed their finger in the car door, they may use Christ's name inappropriately, but probably not Michael Jackson's! Blasphemous language must have a deity to invoke. Despite their allure, reigning celebrities, it seems, lack the *ultimate power* needed for invectives.

Presumption Proscribed

In the third place, this commandment forbids using God's name as a magical formula, a kind of good-luck charm. Certain names carry with them an alluring power. If I were to tell my students that a popular rock music star would appear in the next chapel service, virtually all of them would be vying for seats on the front row. If I were the president's first cousin, all I'd have to do to get first-rate treatment in San Diego would be to mention my kinship with him.

Using powerful names enables one to manipulate things to one's own advantage. So, as Joy Davidman says, "What was prohibited was the misuse of power."[6] Following the Civil War, Gen. Robert E. Lee lost virtually everything. He not only lost the war but also lost property, salary, position in society. He was, however, a war hero—even to many Northerners. Consequently, he was offered a lucrative position with a life insurance company: honorary president for life. The company offered him a good salary for no work. They only wanted to profit from the use of his name. Lee, however, refused the offer, explaining, "Gentlemen, I have nothing left but my name, and that is not for sale."[7]

Too often we want to trade upon God's name, invoking it like magic to achieve our ends. When we're sick, we claim healing in the name of Jesus, acting as if He's obligated to answer our prayer. When we're poor, we pray for wealth in the name of Jesus, assuming He's as frantic about our finances as we are. We use God's name, we use His Son Jesus' name, as if they were magical "open sesame" tools with which to gain our own desires. That's taking God's name in vain—and we who teach and preach are often among the worst offenders of the third commandment.

Still more, perhaps most important, this commandment condemns frivolous religious rhetoric, talking and using God's name in empty, vain, silly ways—ways that in fact discount the reality of His presence. We can, strangely enough, talk about God in such a way as to indicate we really don't think He's here. We can pray, using God's name, in ways that indicate we really don't think there's a divine Person who hears and weighs our words.

And that's especially true for God-talk. We religious folks often get inoculated against the awe of our Subject, God! We become numbed to the majesty of what we proclaim. We fall into the trap of using religious language and the name of God to add some special allure to ourselves. Even worse, we easily use words to shape God into our own image—or an image acceptable to us.

Vegetarians envision a vegetarian God; pacifists construct an antiwar God. "There can hardly be a more evil way of taking God's name in vain than this way of presuming to speak in it," Joy Davidman asserts. "For here is spiritual pride, the ultimate sin, in action—the sin of believing in one's own righteousness."[8] So doing, I fear it's clear that we break the third commandment.

Years ago *Leadership Magazine* published a heartrending story, "When AIDS Invades the Pastor's Family," by Doug Herman. In 1985, after complications delivering their first child, his wife required two units of blood. Tragically, the blood was tainted with the HIV-III virus, which often precedes AIDS. Struggling with the issue, Doug claimed biblical promises for healing, telling his wife, "You've already been healed. When the infectious blood entered your body, it was seared clean by the healing touch of Jesus! 'They shall drink any deadly poison and it shall not harm them.' [See Mark 16:18.] That includes blood."

Knowing they were innocent of wrongdoing, giving themselves to pastoral ministry, the Hermans ignored doctors' advice and used no contraceptives, in time conceiving another child. That child tragically came into the world afflicted with AIDS and subsequently died. As Herman told the story, in his brokenness, he confessed his sorrow at *presuming* on God's power, at *assuming* he could somehow bend God's resources to his personal ends.[9]

NEW TESTAMENT INTERNALIZATION: HOW TO HALLOW GOD'S NAME

A century ago Mark Twain talked with a ruthless businessman, one of the robber barons who ruled over the Gilded Age, who piously proclaimed, "Before I die I mean to make a pilgrimage to the Holy Land. I will climb Mount Sinai and read the Ten Commandments aloud at the top," to which Twain replied, "I have a better idea. You could stay home in Boston and keep them."[10] Say what you mean. Mean what you say. Walk your talk!

Over 50 years ago a Texas congressman, Maury Maverick, coined the word "gobbledygook." He said, "Perhaps I was thinking of the old bearded turkey gobbler back in Texas who was always gobbledy gobbling and strutting with ludicrous pomposity. At the end of this gobble, there was a sort of gook." To illustrate "gobbledygook," Maverick cited bureaucratic memos and political manifestos that seem designed to misguide. Against such perversions of our language former Congressman Maverick protested: "A man's language is a very important part of his conduct. He should be held morally responsible for his words just as he is accountable for his other acts."[11]

That isn't new news. Just as we know trees by their fruit, Jesus said, so too we know persons by their words: "The good man brings good things out of the good stored up in him, and the evil man brings evil things out of the evil stored up in him. But I tell you that men will have to give account on the day of judgment for every careless word they have spoken. For by your words you will be acquitted, and by your words you will be condemned" (Matt. 12:35-37).

Further note Jesus' words in the Sermon on the Mount, in which He said: "Simply let your 'Yes' be 'Yes,' and your 'No,' 'No'; anything beyond this comes from the evil one" (5:37). Say what you mean! Mean what you say!

Dale Bruner comments:

> All speech that moves beyond the clear yes or no has its source in the devil. This yes or no clarity also means that there is something devilish about all pedantic or painted speech that seeks to impress with its learning, cleverness, or even devotion. The devil is the author of both extremely abstruse and of extremely pious speech. . . .
>
> Jesus means here, first of all, that speech that goes beyond yes or no simplicity is speech infected by the Evil One.[12]

Most of us share Homer's ancient view, voiced in the *Iliad:* "I detest that man who / hides one thing in the depths of his heart, / and speaks forth another."[13] With Homer, Jesus detested phony speech. He condemned the practice, so common in His day, of religious doublespeak. By manipulating their words, folks eluded responsibility for their promises or statements. They were like some kids I knew as a child—if they crossed their fingers behind their back, they were free to lie.

Shortly before his death Joseph Stalin had a furious argument during the meeting of the presidium. Fuming with anger, Stalin jumped to his feet and collapsed unconscious on the floor. The shocked comrades stared at Stalin's apparently dead body. Then Lavrenty Beria, head of the feared secret police, leaped from his seat and danced around the body, shouting, "We're free at last! Free at last!" At that point Stalin's daughter entered the room and knelt beside him. Suddenly the dictator moved and opened one eye. Seeing this, Beria immediately fell on his knees, took Stalin's hand, and fervently kissed it.[14] Hypocrisy!

It's not too hard to find examples of hypocrisy. What's truly difficult is to correct it in ourselves. To say simply what you mean and mean what you say takes courage and discipline. Especially in the academic setting, where I work, we use words so incessantly that it's easy to play verbal games simply to avoid taking a stand and making our convictions known.

I sometimes catch myself, while answering a student's question, adding item to item, moving from one qualification to another, suddenly realizing I've almost forgotten the question and have little clue as to whether or not I answered it. Our high-powered professorial talk is often a smoke screen, something to hide behind to avoid stating what we think.

We've probably all had teachers who never admitted to making a mistake. It's tough—when you're supposed to know something (allegedly the reason you're teaching)—to admit you don't know what you're supposed to know. But if we speak Jesus' way, we simply say, "I don't know."

One of my friends attended a very scholarly lecture, filled with abstract language and heavy intellectual content. When he got home, his wife asked him how the lecture had gone.

"Fine," he said.

"Well," she continued, "what did he say?"

Forced to think about it, he replied: "Beats me." That's telling the truth—admitting he didn't understand.

When we deploy language as a smoke screen to evade responsibility for our actions, or our promises, we become hypocrites. When we play verbal games to avoid truth about ourselves, we play the game of hypocrisy. And nothing more quickly separates us from God than verbal games—especially of the religious sort—pretending we are what we're not.

In 1877 a minor conflict erupted into a full-scale war between the Nez Percé and the United States Army in Oregon. Trying to escape the conflict, Chief Joseph and a few hundred people several times defeated an army many times larger. Finally, worn out by fighting and hunger, Chief Joseph agreed to surrender, accepting a treaty that he judged fair. Thereafter, however, the treaty was ignored and the Nez Percé mistreated. Summing up his dealings with the United States, Chief Joseph said:

> I have heard talk and talk, but nothing is done. Good words do not last long unless they amount to something. Words do not pay for my dead people. They do not pay for my country, now overrun by white men. . . . Good words will not give my people good health and stop them from dying. Good words will not get my people a home where they can live in peace and take care of themselves. I am tired of talk that comes to nothing. It makes my heart sick when I remember all the good words and broken promises.[15]

No wonder many American Indians declared, "White man speaks with forked tongue." I wonder how often we too speak with forked tongues! How often do our words mislead rather than enlighten? Are we talking Jesus' way?

Humans have talked and named things from the beginning. We have the unique ability to define things, describe things, name things. And we need to do it with care.

Names Really Matter—and Ought to Be Hallowed

Names matter! The names we call one another mean something. Though this is true, some folks treat them frivolously. Some parents almost seem to delight in discomforting their kids by giving them strange names. We once lived beside a couple who named their three boys Tom, Dick, and Harry. Some parents with the last name of Stone named their son Roland, perhaps to commemorate the Bob Dylan classic song "Rolling Stone." Folks who hang labels such as Crystal Shanda Lear on their kids have no notion of the potential damage done thereby.

Some folks dislike their names enough to get them legally changed. An Arizona Indian asked a judge to give him a shorter name. "What's your name now?" asked the judge.

"Chief Screeching Train Whistle," the Indian replied.

"And to what do you wish to shorten it?" asked the judge.

Standing a bit taller, folding his arms across his chest, Chief Screeching Train Whistle solemnly said: "Toots."

If that story were true (and it's not), "Toots" needed to study his tribal history a bit more. For Indian peoples, especially those lacking written languages, believed that names revealed the essence of what was named. Thus, young Indians, as they entered adolescence, often took names that came to them in visions, names that indicated who they were and what they aspired to become. When, as a young boxer, Cassius Clay converted to Islam and changed his name to Muhammad Ali, he made an important statement. He was saying that his name should reveal his inner essence, stand for his true identity.

If you respect Muhammad Ali—or even if you just want to stay healthy—you'd be wise never to call him Cassius Clay. His name identifies his new character as a Muslim. So too we reveal our respect for God when we rightly use, when we "hallow," His name, His real nature, God as He is. The names we use referring to God mean something. So Jesus, teaching His disciples to pray, said to begin by saying, "Our Father . . . *Hallowed* be Thy *name*. . . . on earth as it is in heaven" (Matt. 6:9-10, NASB, emphases added).

The Greek word *hagiasthētō* means to treat as holy, to use reverently, to sanctify. The word is best translated, Frederick Dale Bruner says, as asking God to make himself *central* to us.[16] We ask God to reveal himself to us so that we may see Him as He really is, that we may know Him in a deeply personal way.

How to Hallow a Name

We hallow God's name when we give Him our *mind's attention*. When God's name is mentioned, we turn attentive. If a noted athlete such as Michael Jordan came to the campus where I teach, young athletes would congregate and listen carefully to everything he said. They would long just to be near him, hoping to absorb some of his talents.

Now God speaks to us through His Word—the written word of Scripture and the crafted word of creation. If we're interested in a loving relationship with the living God, we need to be attentive to His voice. In the perceptive words of C. S. Lewis:

> We may ignore, but we can nowhere evade, the Presence of God. The world is crowded with Him. He walks everywhere incognito. And the incognito is not always hard to penetrate. The real labor is to attend. In fact, to come awake. Still more, to remain awake.[17]

We also pray that God's will will become so central to us that He ignites our *heart's affection*. I rather agree with the great theologian Jonathan Edwards, who insisted, in the midst of America's First Great Awakening, that a warm heart, as well as an enlightened mind, characterizes authentic Christians. Without strong affections, without impassioned love, we fall short of Jesus' call. We need holy affections!

I'm not a very emotional person. I usually just plod along, on an even keel, rarely feeling particularly high or low. Some of you no doubt are saying, "Dull, dull, dull!" Given my temperament, I've never particularly trusted highly emotional religious expressions. I frequently quote to myself one of Martin Luther's poems that says:

> *Feelings come, and feelings go,*
> *And feelings are deceiving.*
> *My warrant is the Word of God,*
> *Naught else is worth believing.*[18]

I think that's true. My faith is focused on God and His Word, not my emotional state.

Yet some things do in fact warm my heart. I rather regularly feel some things. Twenty years ago, in fact, I was moved to tears by a race: the 10,000-meter race in the Olympics at Tokyo. A virtually unknown American runner, Billy Mills, who was not even considered one of this country's elite, much less the best in the world, won that race. And I was deeply moved as I watched him win. My heart was warmed because I knew Billy's story—a poor young Sioux who had overcome incredible odds to make it to the Olympics and win that race. So too, when I see Jesus on the Cross, when I see Him living as He did, my heart is warmed. His name is hallowed in the hollow of my heart.

We also hallow God's name when we give Him our *lips' adoration*. We pray that He will reveal himself so as to elicit our praise. Whenever we see something truly awesome, we cannot keep from praising it. We clap or cheer or say complimentary things when we're impressed.

To see adoration in action, all you need to do is to listen to some of the introductions given celebrities on television and the audience response to their appearance. They're called the "greatest," the "finest," the "most talented." Their words are warmly received, and questions to them are almost always most reverential. We adore our stars and show it. We give standing ovations to celebrities, whether or not their performances deserve it.

Well, if God is like Jesus, if the Bible properly portrays God, nothing short of adoration is in order. In the Book of Revelation, John reports that around the throne of God there is endless adoration. Four heavenly beasts "rest not day and night, saying, Holy, holy, holy, Lord God Almighty, which was, and is, and is to come" (4:8, KJV). Then "the four and twenty elders fall down before him that sat on the throne, and worship him that liveth for ever and ever, and cast their crowns before the throne, saying, Thou art worthy, O Lord, to receive glory and honour and power: for thou hast created all things, and for thy pleasure they are and were created" (vv. 10-11, KJV).

We love a person by hallowing, keeping central, his or her name. We really want to know the person as he or she is, to relate rightly to him or her.

Several years ago while driving down the road, I actually thought of a new subject for conversation with my wife. Not long after you get married, you run out of new subjects to discuss! But I thought of a new one. I asked my wife, Roberta, if she liked her name. She said no, not really—that she had never much liked her name.

She's the second child in her family, and since the firstborn was a girl, her parents had expected a boy—and planned to name him Robert. Instead, a little girl arrived. So they named her Roberta. She's never particularly liked the name, in part because it sounds old-fashioned and out-dated, whereas she's a very up-to-date, stylish woman.

Then I asked her what she wished her name was. She thought a moment, then said, "Trixie."

"*Trixie!*" I said. It's quite a revelation to find that your wife of 15 years secretly thinks she's a "Trixie." So I said I didn't think I could handle "Trixie" and asked her what her second choice would be.

She thought a moment, then said: "Rob."

So from that moment onward I've called her Rob. For a few years she unsuccessfully tried to get friends and family to follow suit, but only a few could make the adjustment. Now she has relapsed and uses the name "Roberta." But I still call her "Rob." Because that's the name (next to Trixie, I guess) she thinks best describes her.

So too with God. We call Him by names that adequately describe Him. We hallow His name by using it well, asking that He reveal himself to us as He really is so as to evoke our attention, our affection, our adoration.

6

A Sanctified Cosmos

OLD TESTAMENT FOUNDATION: LIVING SABBATICALLY

Loving bonds stay strong as nourished by goodly amounts of good time together. Children need parents to spend time with them. That is the only way they can share their *being*. Husbands and wives too often lose their love for each other by losing touch, speeding along their separate ways. Life together requires time together.

What's true for human relationships certainly applies to our walk with God; so to help us focus on the quality of our experience with the Lord, it's helpful on a regular basis to ask ourselves this important question: "Are we finding any ecstasy in life's monotony?" Emily Dickinson wrote:

> *Take all from me, but leave me Ecstasy,*
> *And I am richer than all my Fellow men.*[1]

To prepare us for such, the Scripture calls us to *sabbatical living*.

For a few years my wife taught high school in a small country town where you might expect old-time 4-H Club virtues to prevail. However, her kids seemed as bent on partying and self-destruction as urban adolescents in California. One morning she overheard an amazing conversation. On the previous night a bunch of the kids had staged a beer bash at a lake, and one girl got so smashed that she passed out midway through the party. The next morning she couldn't remember what happened. So she asked her friends (who were laughing at the way she had handled her liquor) this question: "Did I have a good time?" Now I think, since she had to ask the question, she probably didn't. Surely part of having a good time is being able to remember it!

This girl had expected to find a good time in sensual pleasures. It's an old temptation, what Latin church fathers called *concupiscence,* the pleasures or lusts of the flesh. Such pleasures pass quickly and leave us hangovers and heartaches, hardly making our lifetime good. We're also tempted to imagine that we'll settle into the good life when we finally collect enough possessions to feel secure. Such temptation the early fathers called *covetousness.* Yet neither pleasures nor possessions make time good, for the thing that makes time good is a quality of being—good living rather than having goods.

I'm persuaded that "good time" means a quality of experience, a goodness of being. It's better to be than to do or to have. This is the abiding truth of biblical Sabbaths, for the Bible reminds us that we need to stop work, to relax, to simply *be* the persons God made us to be. Could we but learn to live at ease—sabbatically—we might learn to prefer being to having.

In that way we would imitate to a small degree our Heavenly Father. Here Scripture provides us a divine example to follow. We are to live just as God lives—at ease, resting—sabbatically. To live sabbatically means, primarily, awakening to an acute awareness of God in creation.

The creation story says God rested on the seventh day. He wasn't tired. He didn't need to catch His breath. He rested to enjoy what He had made. Having blessed His creatures, God chose to reflect upon, to interact with, to appreciate His work. God freely created, which is to say He created out of love, making a world of goodness and glory.

Truly my wife's student's question touches on a deeper question: *What makes time good?* How can we make our time good? Lots of us neither tolerate nor manage time well. In the morning we can't wait for the day to pass. On Monday we can't wait for the weekend. At the beginning of the school term we can't wait for it to end. We'd often prefer not to be conscious of the dull routines of life—the minutes and hours and days of study and work, of traffic and tasks.

For many folks, the dullness of daily routines leads to the frantic party times lauded by beer commercials. Some folks survive the day because they look forward to the "happy hour." Some endure the week in hopes of a weekend fling. Obviously they aren't solely interested in sitting down and having meaningful conversations. They want an excuse to drink. How interesting that people drink beer, or vodka, to get intoxicated—when the very word "intoxicate" means to ingest poison!

I doubt people get drunk because they admire drunks, for drunks behave in bizarre ways. There's a story about a man who left a party where he had more than enough booze. Outside the watering hole he spotted a uniformed man who looked like a doorman and said, "Would you get me a taxi, my good man?"

In response, the uniformed man straightened his back and retorted: "See here—I happen to be a rear admiral in the United States Navy."

"Perfectly all right," said the drunk. "Just get me a battleship then."

Though I don't approve of drunkenness, I think I understand why people drink. They find life boring and want to escape the dullness of time. Intoxication lifts one, if only for a few hours, out of the deadness of daily routines. So too do diversions of various sorts, insulators from time's reality.

The idea that time should, at least sometimes, be good is the central truth of one of the distinctive marks of Judaism: the biblical Sabbath. The Bible reminds us that we need to stop work, to take it easy, to simply *be* and to enjoy being the persons God desires us to be. If we can learn to live at ease sabbatically, we'll come to prefer being to having. So hear the Word of the Lord: "Remember the Sabbath day by keeping it holy. Six days you shall labor and do all your work, but the seventh day is a Sabbath to the LORD your God. On it you shall not do any work. . . . For in six days the LORD made the heavens and the earth . . . but he rested on the seventh day. Therefore the LORD blessed the Sabbath day and made it holy" (Exod. 20:8-11).

Regarding this text, the great Jewish scholar Abraham Joshua Heschel wrote: "Judaism is a *religion of time,* aiming at the *sanctification of time.*"[2] I would add that not only personally does God want to sanctify us, but also through us He wants to sanctify His world.

God's Example

The creation account reveals God rested on the seventh day. He wasn't all worn out with exertion. He didn't need to rest up. He rested in order to *enjoy* what He had made. Having called into being creatures both good and beautiful, God determined to view, to interact with, to appreciate His work. He created and delighted in creation. He's present in His handiwork, wanting to be with and to enjoy the beauty and goodness of His world.

"Creation is God's work," writes Jürgen Moltmann, "but the sabbath is God's present existence. His works express God's will, but the sabbath manifests his Being."[3] Today we need an acute awareness of God in creation. We need to discern His reality through the stillness of sabbatical living, hearing (as did Elijah on Mount Horeb, the mountain of God) the One who softly whispers out of the surrounding silences.

I'm not a professional builder, but when I make things, I rather like to step back and admire my work when I'm done. I once laid some ceramic tile in our town house. Often after finishing a section, I'd stand back, eye it, and inwardly say, "That's good! I like that."

Now a skilled craftsman might look at my job and force himself to mumble, "Well—not bad." But I took delight in my accomplishment.

When we make something, we don't just forget it—we want to stay in touch with, to be present with what we've made. So I still enjoy walking barefoot on the tile I laid. It just pleases me by being there. In the sense that I attribute worth to it, I have a worshipful attitude.

There's a profound difference between work time and worship time. The Greeks, whose language was often quite precise, distinguished between *chronos,* the ticking clock time we work by, and *kairos,* a suspended-animation, reflective time. *Chronos* time is necessary, inescapable. But like the tick, tick, tick of the clock, it's *monotonous*—one dull tone after another. Can you imagine anything duller than listening to an endlessly ticking clock?

Kairos, however, is time with a melody, at times an *ecstasy,* when we slip through a "wrinkle in time" and enter another dimension wherein clock time disappears. We discover when we experience both kinds of time that *kairos* is really *good* time. We need points of *ecstasy* to lighten up life's *monotony.*

Amazingly enough, time is really good when we lose consciousness of it. One sure measure of a good time is this: you never check your watch when you're having a good time. (This, I must admit, worries me a lot as I teach and preach and see people shaking their watches, staring in disbelief.) I've heard a few sermons that lifted me above time—I didn't want them to end. And I've heard lectures that seemed as if they would never end. (We professors have the great advantage of *giving* lots of lectures rather than *enduring* them. And I tell you the Bible is right when it says it's more blessed to give than to receive.)

I've read books I wished wouldn't end. In fact, I have at times limited myself to a certain number of pages a day so as to delay reaching the end. And then I've read all too many books that I thought would never end! I forced myself to a few pages a day in these just because that's all I could endure. I understand why editors have a shorthand formula for books they reject—"MEGO": My Eyes Glass Over!

What I find in those times that I find good is a joyous delight, an ecstasy in the present moment that opens a "wrinkle in time" to eternity. For, as C. S. Lewis asks: "Where, except in the present, can the Eternal be met?"[4]

God's Exhortation

Not only did God rest on the seventh day, but also He commanded His people to remember the Sabbath, to make it holy. To sustain a covenant bond with God, we need to devote *time* to Him. We all know it's necessary to reserve time for those we love if we want to stay in love. So the fourth commandment is a prescription for keeping love alive.

Rightly read, the Old Testament calls for three different kinds of Sabbath: one day out of seven, one year out of seven, and a culminating jubilee year to consummate a 50-year cycle. For the truth about reality is this: while work's necessary, it's not the *one thing* necessary. "Man does not live on bread alone," Jesus said in Luke 4:4. Work must be kept in its rightful place: integrated with, merely a part of, our *being* the *persons* we're called to be.

If I want to maintain a good marriage, I must spend time with my wife. In fact, the very best thing I can spend on my wife is my time. Quite frankly, my idea of a good time is sitting quietly at home, reading and enjoying an evening with my wife. Almost nothing (neither concerts, nor ball games, nor parties) much appeals to me once the sun sets.

And when I'm home enjoying my wife's presence, I'm unconcerned with the clock. In fact, when the evening ends and it's time to retire, I often wonder how the time slipped so quickly away! That's because I enjoy just being with my wife. And I enjoy being in the home she makes, for she is, among other things, a marvelous homemaker. To live with my wife means to relax and enjoy her presence in the world she has created.

What's true for my marriage is also true for my life in God. For me to know and enjoy God's presence, the main investment I must make is simply to take time for Him. Taking time to be with Him means relaxing and enjoying His world, His creation, the good earth and its plants and animals, its mountains and oceans. If I do so, perhaps I'll begin to see things from His perspective and live wisely and well. Perhaps I'll learn to *live sabbatically.*

To do this means we'll need to stop the compulsive busyness that characterizes our normal routines. We need to slow down! Will Rogers observed, "Half our life is spent trying to find something to do with the time we have rushed through life trying to save."[5] Centuries earlier Geoffrey Chaucer wrote, "Great peace is found in little busyness." One of the great missionary statesmen of an earlier day had a motto in his office that said: "Beware of the barrenness of a busy life." How true! Too often our lives are barren because they're fixated on the furious quest to make money and get more things. We need simply to stop and be God's children, husbands of wives, moms and dads with time for their kids, folks who enjoy picnics and walks in woods, simple activities that add nothing to our bank accounts.

Lots of folks in our society take off work at least one day a week (though their "rest" may not approximate the biblical model). But the second sabbatical commanded in Scripture—resting for an entire year—is almost nowhere practiced. In a technological society it probably can't be observed. But if we want to follow God's plan for man, we need to follow its call to *ease off*, to reduce our consumption so as to conserve creation.

God commanded His people to rest every seventh year, plus a jubilee every 50 years, to let creation take a rest as well. The land needs a rest. Plants and animals need time to flourish freely without man's demands. Were this universally practiced, we would have far fewer ecological worries. Earth's soil is a marvelous organic mix of living creatures. Since farming wearies the soil, it needs periodic rest and restoration. James Houston says, "More than anything else the Sabbath rest symbolizes man's awareness of living in God's creation"[6]—which means *living sabbatically!*

One of the great Christians in our world is Paul Brand, a missionary doctor in India, where he pioneered some techniques to deal with leprosy. He now works in a leprosy hospital in Louisiana. Looking back over his life's investment as a missionary doctor, and looking at the current environmental degradation in India, Brand fears the very wellsprings of life may have been destroyed. While he's been tending needy lepers, the land has been despoiled. He recently said, "I would gladly give up medicine and surgery tomorrow if by so doing I could have some influence on policy with regard to mud and soil. The world will die from lack of soil and pure water long before it will die from lack of antibiotics or surgical skill and knowledge."[7]

Now God created, delighted in, is present in, wants to be with, and enjoys the beauty and goodness of His world. I suspect God's a bit like the people who gather to watch Old Faithful perform every hour in Yellowstone National Park. I've joined the crowd a number of times, and when the geyser shoots upward, we always applaud. I doubt Old

Faithful particularly cares, but we who see its performance so delight in it that we can't fail to clap our hands.

I imagine God continually applauds the beauty of His handiwork here on earth. And we're invited to join Him, to discover the ecstasy of enjoying the beauty and goodness of creation.

NEW TESTAMENT INTERNALIZATION: A NEW DAY FOR THE NEW WAY

Years ago my wife and I took one of my nephews to church with us. Because of the size of the crowds, the Sunday evening service was televised on a big screen in an overflow auditorium, where we went with Travis. Later, when his folks came to get him, they asked what he had done. He said, "We saw a movie at church—but it wasn't very good."

I suspect lots of folks drop out of church because it's not very good. It's dull rather than delightful. Going to church becomes something "you gotta do" rather than a place you long to go in order to meet a special Someone. Consequently, one of the first things many college students do, free from the restrictions of home, is to stop attending church. Since it's not what some define as "a good time," many folks just ignore the fourth of the Ten Commandments and fail to find what is God's good time.

While looking at the Ten Commandments, I've tried to move between the Old Testament Law and the New Testament's internalization of that law. The Sabbath commandment, at first glance, seems an exception to that pattern, for the New Testament says little about it. Yet if we see that the Sabbath was given to lift us into God's time, to help us find some out-of-time ecstasy amid the routines of life, the New Testament has something even better for us than the Old Testament's seventh-day observance.

When you read the New Testament, you discover that Jesus had little concern for rigid Sabbath restrictions. In fact, He routinely got in trouble for His Sabbath activities. Mark's Gospel records one such incident, in which Jesus was condemned because His disciples had picked some grain in a field. Jesus responded that David, though not a priest, had entered God's house and eaten "consecrated bread" reserved for priests because he needed to eat. Then He declared: "The Sabbath was made for man, not man for the Sabbath. So the Son of Man is Lord even of the Sabbath" (2:27-28).

We're Not Made for the Sabbath

Sabbath observance, for many people in Jesus' day, had degenerated into an almost endless list of prohibitions. Some contemporary church folks, if reared by conservative parents in conservative congregations, are tempted to think they lived under too many rules. But compared to the ancient Pharisees, virtually all American Evangelicals are quite permissive!

Back then learned rabbis had taken the fourth of the Ten Commandments, "Remember the sabbath day, to keep it holy" (Exod. 20:8, KJV), and figured out 39 classes, with 39 subclasses under each class of forbidden work—1,521 different tasks or activities. A farmer couldn't sow seeds or plow fields or harvest grain. A homemaker couldn't light a fire or put out a fire, knead dough or bake bread. You couldn't tie a knot or untie a knot. This, I note, would perfectly suit some of my students, who trudge about with perennially untied shoelaces.

As you might expect, these prohibitions led to some curious interpretations. For one thing, Sabbath spitting was forbidden. The Pharisees reasoned one ought not spit on the Sabbath because the man who did so might carelessly rub it with his sandal and create a ball of dirt—and that would be plowing on the Sabbath!

Some rabbis declared that you could feed chickens on the Sabbath, but you must feed them vegetables or bread, not grain, because the chickens might miss a kernel and bury it while scratching around—and then you would have sowed seed on the Sabbath. You were allowed to use a mirror during the week, but on Saturday, the Sabbath, you couldn't use it—for you'd be tempted to pluck out an errant hair in your eyebrow or beard, and that would be harvesting on the Sabbath (though why anyone would "harvest" hair is beyond my understanding). If you had a wooden leg and your house caught fire, you couldn't put out the fire, but you could flee to safety—however, you had to leave your wooden leg behind, because it's wrong to haul wood on the Sabbath.

To the Pharisees, then, Jesus' disciples did a multitude of wrongs. In a matter of moments they broke every rule! Plucking the heads of wheat from the stalks, they "harvested" it; rubbing it between their hands to get the kernels, they "threshed" it; separating the grain from the chaff, they "winnowed" it; and in the process they "prepared a meal"—four forms of work forbidden on the Sabbath.

Now if Sabbath restrictions merely limited one's fun, perhaps they'd be inconsequential and tolerable. But they actually subverted God's intent by making the Sabbath a kind of duty time when you kept Him happy. Rather than Sabbath being a special time, a sacred time when God's presence could be better discerned, it became a time when He was kept afar, securely in His judgment seat. Rather than liberating one from hard labor so as to enjoy God's good world, Sabbath had become a prison with walls of time wherein nothing enjoyable could be done. So, while trying to do a good thing, keeping the Sabbath holy, many of Jesus' contemporaries made life miserable for men and women who needed a day of rest. Men and women need a joyous day, but the Pharisees reduced it to a heavy routine of prohibitions.

A New Day for the New Way

Immediately after Pentecost, as soon as Christians be-gan celebrating a "new way"—Jesus' way—they began cel-ebrating a new day, the Lord's day. Though most of His disciples were Jews, they quickly substituted the Lord's day (Sunday) for the Sabbath (Saturday). "On the first day of the week," Luke says, "we came together to break bread" (Acts 20:7). Accurately speaking, Christians don't observe the "Sabbath," the seventh day of the week. Chris-tians celebrate God's Son's day, Sunday, the first day of the week—or the eighth day, as some prefer to say.

Living in the Roman Empire, early Christians faced a society that didn't grant them Sundays off; so Sunday, the Lord's day, was hardly a Jewish-style day of rest. For cen-turies Christians met (often early in the morning before go-ing about required routines) and rejoiced on the Lord's day, for it helped them remember the Resurrection. *Jesus is Lord—and He is risen!* The Lord's day is the day to remem-ber His resurrection.

Thus, one of the Apostolic Fathers, Ignatius of Anti-och, on his way to Rome to be executed, wrote, "No longer observe the Jewish Sabbaths, but keep holy the Lord's day, on which, through Him and through His death, our life arose."[8] Somewhat later Athanasius, a fourth-century fa-ther, noted that Christians kept "no Sabbaths," observing instead "the Lord's Day as a memorial of the beginning of the new creation."[9]

Celebrating creation, old and new, on the first day of the week—that's the new day for the new way of Christ. Reducing Sunday to "time served," a *duty* to be grudging-ly endured, perverts the good news of Christ's gospel.

I heard a story about a little boy who saw a plaque hanging in his church's foyer, dedicated to the memory of soldiers who had died in the war. He asked, "Who are the people whose names are on the plaque?"

An adult responded: "Those are the names of the men who died in the service."

Instantly interested, the little guy said: "Really? In which service—9:30 or 11:00?"

Admittedly, sometimes our worship services are more dead than alive, more boring than uplifting. But they ought not be. They should celebrate the resurrection of the Lord Jesus. *Jesus is Lord, and He is risen!*—that was the motto of the Early Church. So each Sunday believers came together to rejoice, just to be happy in the realization of who Jesus is, to enjoy the reality of His presence. More than anything else, Sunday should be a *good time* for us, for we know that in Jesus we have entered into *eternal life*, God's timeless time.

I have the privilege to preach regularly in the chapels where I serve as chaplain and in churches and retreats. Many things concern me: orthodox doctrine, commitment to Christ, ethical living. But as much as anything else, when I preach, I'd like to exude the "joy that Jesus gives." The Sabbath's goal, to restore something of the peace and joy of the Garden of Eden, certainly should be central in celebrating the Lord's day. For as Augustine said: "There is a joy that is not given unto the wicked, but to those who freely worship Thee, whose joy Thou Thyself art. . . . For a happy life is joy in the truth; and this is joy in Thee, who art the Truth."[10]

The Lord's day also looks forward to a great day coming, a glorious day when the saints and angels will all be perfected in the ecstasy of heaven. So Sunday, the Lord's day, not only is the first day of the week but also signifies the new creation—the eighth day—that God will establish through Jesus Christ. He's "the author and perfecter of our faith" (Heb. 12:2), and each Lord's day we gather to remember joyously His coming—and His coming again.

I love to read the works of C. S. Lewis, including his

Chronicles of Narnia. In *The Voyage of the "Dawn Treader,"* in which the voyagers, Prince Caspian and his hardy band, sail through the "wonders of the last sea" to "the very end of the world," the reader senses the joy of life embraced as an adventure. The book ends as the knightly little mouse, Reep-a-cheep, steps off the boat, determined to go over the edge of the sea in his quest for Aslan. Caught up by Lewis's artistry, I inwardly rejoiced to *feel* momentarily ecstatic at what I know: we're created not just for time but for eternity. This world, for all its goodness and beauty, is not our final home.

Thus "the Beloved Disciple," John, declared: "I was in the Spirit on the Lord's day" (Rev. 1:10, KJV). Then he closes his Revelation with this vision:

> And I saw a new heaven and a new earth: for the first heaven and the first earth were passed away; and there was no more sea. And I John saw the holy city, new Jerusalem, coming down from God out of heaven, prepared as a bride adorned for her husband. And I heard a great voice out of heaven saying, Behold, the tabernacle of God is with men, and he will dwell with them, and they shall be his people, and God himself shall be with them, and be their God. And God shall wipe away all tears from their eyes; and there shall be no more death, neither sorrow, nor crying, neither shall there be any more pain: for the former things are passed away. And he that sat upon the throne said, Behold, I make all things new. And he said unto me, Write: for these words are true and faithful. And he said unto me, It is done. I am Alpha and Omega, the beginning and the end. I will give unto him that is athirst of the fountain of the water of life freely. He that overcometh shall inherit all things; and I will be his God, and he shall be my son *(21:1-7, KJV).*

A few years after we married, my wife and I started a tradition that we religiously observe. Each Saturday morning we go out for breakfast. These days in San Diego we usually walk two miles to our favorite breakfast spot, enjoy a good meal, and walk home. Sometimes, when one of us is out of town, we miss our Saturday morning date. But when we're together, we always go out for breakfast.

Now we don't say much as we walk along. Sometimes we even read sections of the Saturday paper in the café. I don't suppose you'd say we're *ecstatic* about anything in particular. But it's something we both look forward to. I think I can say our weekly breakfast is an important part of the joy that makes our marriage rich and rewarding. By being together, by taking time just to be present with one another, we make it clear we're committed to sharing life together. It's *good* time, because it's commitment time that makes our relationship *good*.

So, too, I think Sundays, the Lord's days, give us regular times, appointed hours, when we make it clear we're committed to sharing life with Him. *Sunday is God's Son's day!* It's a time when we rejoice in His presence. It's a time when the new covenant is consecrated by sacred time. We take seriously the admonition in Hebrews: "Not neglecting to meet together" (10:25, NRSV).

7

The Sanctity
of the Family

OLD TESTAMENT FOUNDATION:
HONOR YOUR FATHER AND MOTHER

Some of us think our parents are the greatest folks in the world, and we hope to be just like them. Others of us can hardly stand our parents, so we work hard all our life trying to be utterly unlike them. Some of us "sorta" like our folks but wish they would grow up or come down to earth. Some of us couldn't wait to escape the confines of home, to get away from our parents, only to discover quickly we wanted nothing more than to return home, to live in the warmth and shelter the folks provide.

On the other hand, some of us might be alarmed to know how our folks felt about *us!* Tensions separating the generations, the generation gap, seem to trouble us forever. Listen to this news item:

> Children now love luxury. They have bad manners, contempt for authority. They show disrespect for elders and love to talk in place of exercise. Children are now tyrants. . . . They no longer rise when an elder enters the room. They contradict their parents, chatter before company, gobble up food at the table, cross their legs and tyrannize their teachers.

Sound like a letter to today's *Los Angeles Times?* In fact, it's an ancient Greek complaint, recorded 2,400 years ago!

Even earlier, some 2,800 years ago, the prophet Micah cataloged the sins of his contemporaries by crying out, "For a son dishonors his father, a daughter rises up against her mother, a daughter-in-law against her mother-in-law— a man's enemies are the members of his own household" (7:6).

Honestly, we have a problem—a big problem. It's a family problem, a problem with the family. If you're concerned about family, your present and future families, think for a few minutes about God's Word for us: "Honor your father and your mother, so that you may live long in the land the Lord your God is giving you" (Exod. 20:12). The fifth commandment extends God's concern for covenant relationships to the most basic social institution—the family. To live rightly with God, to stay in covenant with Him, we need to live rightly with others, beginning at home.

A Matter of Honor: Appreciation

For the good of the family, children must *honor* their parents. The word "honor" doesn't necessarily mean a son must like his father, that a daughter must enjoy being around her mother. It's mainly a matter of *appreciation,* not affection, though there's an incredible amount of natural affection family members share with each other. Honoring doesn't depend on one's parents' attractiveness, intelligence, athletic ability, or financial assets. It's not tied to performance; just as some students forever fail to make the dean's list, so some parents never quite make the list of "the world's top 10 parents." I wish all our parents were winners, but they're not. But we must see how it's possible to honor our parents without particularly admiring them.

The fifth commandment means parents deserve something just because they're parents. They're to be honored because of what they've done and the position they occupy, not because they're effective. We're to honor our parents just because they *are* our parents, not because they're the kind of parents we would like them to be. Primarily this means we honor them for giving us the most priceless of all gifts: life.

More than 30 years ago the *Milwaukee Sentinel* conducted a contest titled "My Pop's Tops," encouraging children to nominate their dads for the prize. One of the entries declaimed: "Every child should love their father because if it was not for their father where would they be? Nowhere, that's where they'd be. If it was not for fathers you wouldn't see hardly no children around Milwaukee."

And that's true—without fathers, none of us would be. Kids need parents simply to get here. Just as God's covenant with His people grew out of His most basic self-revelation, "I AM WHO I AM" (Exod. 3:14, a truth that ought to elicit our deepest gratitude), so too our covenant with our parents grows out of the very basic truth that they gave us life. Without them we'd just not be.

I appreciate my mother, for she carried me in her womb and birthed me, even though I remember nothing about her, since she was burned to death when I was three and a half years old. When I meet her someday, I want to say, "Thanks!" I support the ancient Roman philosopher, Seneca, who applauded his mother for refusing to engage in "unchastity, 'the greatest evil of our time,' and for never having 'crushed the hope of children that were being nurtured in her body.'"[1]

Some of you were adopted as babies. Naturally you struggle with the decision of your birth mother or parents to give you away. You've wrestled with feelings many of us can never understand. But in the midst of the most powerful feelings, never forget this: it's good to be alive. And your natural mother and father, however else they failed you, gave you life. Some of you may have been abused as children and wrestle with angry, hateful feelings toward your abusive parents. Such feelings are under-standable, natural, inevitable. But in the midst of your pain, however much they failed you, there's still, for most of you, an inescapable thankfulness for the gift of life—a gift only parents can give.

Some of you have parents who divorced. *You* feel di-vorced as well. You feel what seems to be a depthless ache. To ask you not to feel such pain is like asking a man who has just been stabbed to stop bleeding. Bleeding is a nor-mal, healthy response to injury. Your anger, your discon-tent with your mom or dad, is basically a normal, healthy—at least at one stage—response to injury. But amid the pain, always remember: the most precious gift we've ever received is the gift of life.

So we honor our parents, we *appreciate* them for who they are, the source of our life. Life is precious, even with its pains. Most of us, however harsh our circumstances, love life and seek to prolong it. We have something to pre-serve. We're more than *nothing*, thanks to our parents!

A Necessary Chain of Command: Authority!

In honoring our father and mother, we also acknowl-edge and try to fit into God's plan for creation. We may like democracy, and rightly run democratic political sys-tems are admirable. But the universe is no democracy. It's a hierarchy. There's a chain of command, a pyramid of re-sponsibility, built into the very fabric of reality. There is au-thority derived from God that makes creation harmonious, and parents are commissioned monarchs, ordered to guide their little kingdoms under God's divine direction.

To many of us, breathing in an atmosphere that urges us to stake claim to personal autonomy, "authority" sounds like a dirty word. But it has nine letters, so it's too long to be profane! An insightful cartoon portrays some graffiti splashed on a wall, declaring in the first frame, "Question Authority!" The second frame shows a smaller addition: "Says Who?" Good question! For all of us both need and constantly rely upon legitimate authorities.

Too often, of course, we confuse "authority" with "authoritarianism," which is an entirely different issue. A legitimate authority is someone who knows something we need to learn.

I've read every book George Sheehan wrote. He was a medical doctor who was one of the world's elite runners. He knew what makes a good runner. I want to know that. So I read and trust him as an *author*. He's an *authority* for me. He would never have wanted to impose his views on me, as would an authoritarian, but he's an authority I choose to heed, for his advice comes with the stamp of wisdom and experience.

So too with Jesus. After He finished the Sermon on the Mount, "the crowds were amazed at his teaching, because he taught as one who had authority, and not as their teachers of the law" (Matt. 7:28-29). Since Jesus wrote the book of human nature, it's understandable He spoke authoritatively about life. He's no tyrant, no authoritarian, but He's an *authority!* To know how to live, we find in Jesus "the way, the truth, and the life" (John 14:6, KJV).

We need authorities in addition to Jesus, particularly when we're young. We need people who have lived long enough and care deeply enough to help us find our way. So in the family, when it functions as God intended, we find good authority. Better than anyone else, our parents know us. They inscribed our script, for their DNA is literally imprinted in our being. They watched us, more meticulously than anyone else, as we matured. They knew the world we live in that has exerted its influence on us. They witnessed the experiences that helped make us what we are. Honoring our parents means listening to them, following their rules, believing they probably know more than we do, believing they care for us enough to give us good guidance.

When I was in junior high school, some of my friends had motor scooters or small motorcycles. My dad made it clear that I was not even to ride one, much less ask for one. Knowing the reckless abandon with which I rode my bicycle, trying a variety of stunts designed to daily endanger my life, he wisely wanted to keep me from multiplying my miscalculations with motorized power. But one day I had the opportunity to ride one of my friend's scooters and (with all the brilliance you would expect of a 13-year-old) rode it right up the hill in front of our house.

Promptly thereafter my father called me into the basement for a deep, down-to-earth discussion. I had not been spanked for many years, but I sensed a spanking was eminently possible. He reminded me of his prohibition, which I agreed had been clearly promulgated. He asked me if I would forswear riding such machines, to which I readily assented. No spanking ensued, for which I was duly grateful. At the time, I thought he was old-fashioned and narrow-minded. But looking back on it, I'm sure he was wise. I didn't need the open-ended opportunities for self-destruction that a "murder-cycle" would provide.

In learning to accept my parents' authority, I also learned to accept teachers' and preachers' and policemen's and presidents' authority. Such folks aren't always right. Now and then they are misguided, even perverse in their acts. They aren't always up-to-date or up-to-snuff. But they are usually worth heeding, worth listening to, worth following, because they represent the wisdom of our race, the collective wisdom deeper and surer than our own.

Bryce J. Christensen's *Utopia Against the Family: The Problems and Politics of the American Family*[2] provides informed insights as to why families have so struggled to survive in the past three decades. The book's title sums it up: social utopians (many of whom are unmarried or childless) undermine families in vain endeavors to establish perfect societies. Many moderns, T. S. Eliot noted, insist on "dreaming of systems so perfect that no one needs to be good."[3] We have followed social blueprints, such as President Lyndon B. Johnson's "Great Society," and forced people to invest trillions of dollars in pipe dreams that vaporize truly necessary things—moral standards, personal responsibility, family ties.

That many utopians want to abolish the traditional family is everywhere evident. Thus we have organizations such as the American Home Economics Association, declaring families have nothing to do with "'blood, legal ties, adoption, or marriage'" but may be defined as "'two or more persons who share resources, share responsibility for decisions, share values and goals, and have commitment to one another over time.'"[4] Such elastic definitions have been picked up and stretched by the media and politicians. For instance, Mario Cuomo once espoused the conviction that the government must *"be* the family of America."[5] When the word "family" may apply to anything from baseball teams to lesbian lovers to an entire country, there has been *verbicide!*

As divorce and single parenthood shake the traditional family, utopians gain adherents to their cause. One of the causes promoted these days is day care. Parents are urged to place children in daycare facilities in order to maintain their professional careers. Such "child-rearing" facilities are the staple of socialist utopias.

Christensen subjects such factories to a stern review, concluding they threaten the well-being of children. Forty years ago an esteemed psychologist, John Bowlby, studied children in such institutions and concluded that a child needs "'a warm, intimate, and continuous relationship with his mother in which both find satisfaction and enjoyment.' Any child lacking such suffers 'maternal deprivation.'"[6] Bowlby's findings have never been refuted. Problems such as contagious diseases and social maladjustment plague daycare facilities. Day care at its best should be a last-resort decision.

The evidence, like a landfill, slowly piles up. In the judgment of two serious scholars, it is clear that

children who grow up in a household with only one biological parent are worse off, on average, than children who grow up in a household with both of their biological parents, regardless of the parents' race or educational background, regardless of whether the parents are married when the child is born, and regardless of whether the resident parent remarries.[7]

That's the truth! For the good of our kids, parents must be married and stay married. Carefully examining such things as success in school, teenage pregnancies, and job performance, a team of scholars in cautious quantitative terms show that, however Hollywood smirks at them, traditional nuclear families really matter.

What then can be done? Christensen says there's hope, but only if we can recover some fundamental convictions, build upon them, and break the hammerlock the utopians have imposed on some of our cultural institutions. There's an old Ashanti (an African tribe) proverb that says: "The ruin of a nation begins in the homes of its people." Nothing I've studied in history stands more amply evident.

We Americans live in a nation that some observers think is on the verge of ruin. The failure of moms and dads, the divorces and the child abuse, the neglect and disinterest have sorely wounded millions of kids. I'd like to reverse or correct all that, but I can't. I have no magic wand, no wonderful formula for the world. Neither have you.

But all of us can, insofar as possible, begin trying to rebuild the families we're part of. Even those of us who are not parents are children. So we can, each of us, do something about the family. That something begins with learning how to rightly honor, to esteem, our fathers and our

mothers and to submit to legitimate authorities as we en-
counter and live with them as God intended.

NEW TESTAMENT INTERNALIZATION: DOING OUR FATHER'S BUSINESS

Years ago I heard James Dobson tell a story about sitting with a group of strangers in a meeting. The time came
for a coffee break, and the leader of the group asked one
member if he wanted to break for coffee and doughnuts.
Insecure, the guy played it safe and said, "No, not now."
Then the leader went around the room, individually asking individuals if they wanted a break. At last he came to
Dobson, who said enthusiastically, "I sure do." Moving toward the refreshments, he found the rest of the group instantly at his heels, grateful for the break from the lecture.
They couldn't wait for the break they had all declined![8]

Sometimes it takes courage to stand up and act according to what you believe—even if you want no more
than a cup of coffee. Most of us, most of the time, conform
to the crowd around us. Even the most individualistic of us
tends to dress like others our age. None of my students
look like my classmates who graduated from college in
1963. My students look much like their peers. Most of today's youngsters listen to the latest musical hits, not because they are the finest music ever written, but because
they are in vogue with their age-group.

What goes for my students goes for us older folks as
well. We tend to dress alike and share musical preferences.
So I often wonder: Have any of us the courage to stand up
and be counted for what counts? Have any of us dared to
stand alone, doing what's right regardless of what it might
cost? The truth is, if we want to follow Jesus, we'll often
have to stand up and defy those who discourage us from
discipleship. That means, at times, doing what our peers—
and even our parents—disapprove of.

Discipline Demands Decisions

Any decision demands discipline. And decisions determine destiny. So decisions flowing from discipline really matter. They determine if what we do, the lives we live, ultimately matters.

Sometimes, though we honor our parents, in following Jesus we must make decisions that disappoint them, decisions that take us in directions they can't understand. In Luke's Gospel, Jesus' first recorded decision disappointed His parents. Joseph and Mary took Jesus to Jerusalem for the Passover feast, and as they returned to Nazareth, they discovered He wasn't with the extended family. They returned to Jerusalem, where He sat in the Temple, discussing theology, amazing His elders. His "astonished" parents chastised Him for causing them distress. In response, Jesus said: "Why were you searching for me? . . . Didn't you know I had to be in my Father's house?" (2:49). Or, in the words of the King James Version, "Wist ye not that I must be about my Father's business?"

The same Jesus who said He came not to "destroy the law" (Matt. 5:17, KJV), including its admonition to honor our parents, dared in this instance to depart from their control. Accordingly, while we should always honor our parents, following the admonition of the fifth commandment, sometimes we must make decisions they dislike. In deciding to stay and study with the teachers in the Temple, Jesus disappointed His folks, but He made it clear it was necessary at times to please His Heavenly Father rather than His earthly father.

"Nothing is more difficult, and therefore more precious," said Napoléon, "than to be able to decide."[9] He was right. We're routinely paralyzed by uncertainty, doubt, fear. Given the chance, we'll call for more study, to refer the issue to a committee, to hope someone else decides for us. To decide, to make a choice and follow it, takes self-discipline, and disciplined choices may separate us from others, even our parents.

For a Christian, as Dietrich Bonhoeffer said, "One thing is clear: we understand Christ only if we commit ourselves to him in a stark 'Either-Or.' He did not go to the cross to ornament and embellish our life."[10] Too often we would like to add Jesus to our life, like wood filler when finishing furniture, just to smooth out the cracks on the surface. But Jesus is not an add-on luxury. Indeed, as Bonhoeffer insisted, "We are concerned with Christ and nothing else. Let Christ be Christ."[11] Still more: "In Jesus God has said Yes and Amen to it all, and that Yes and Amen is the firm ground on which we stand."[12]

Discipline Demands Determination

The discipline discipleship demands roots itself in a determination to do God's will. In Matthew's Gospel Jesus said:

> Whoever acknowledges me before men, I will also acknowledge him before my Father in heaven. But whoever disowns me before men, I will disown him before my Father in heaven.
>
> Do not suppose that I have come to bring peace to the earth. I did not come to bring peace, but a sword. For I have come to turn "a man against his father, a daughter against her mother, a daughter-in-law against her mother-in-law—a man's enemies will be members of his own household."
>
> Anyone who loves his father or mother more than me is not worthy of me . . . and anyone who does not take his cross and follow me is not worthy of me. Whoever finds his life will lose it, and whoever loses his life for my sake will find it (10:32-39).

The good life Christ provides involves discipline. In fact, I sometimes suspect self-discipline is the one thing necessary to live well. With it we can make it; without it we'll slip and slide from side to side, never really doing anything of substance.

Sophocles wrote long ago in *Antigone:* "If men live decently it is because / discipline saves their very lives for them."[13] More recently Tom Landry, the great former football coach of the Dallas Cowboys, said it this way: "My job is to get men to do what they don't want to do so that they can achieve what they always wanted to achieve."

Most of us know that the difference between a child and an adult boils down to this: adults do what's *worthwhile*, knowing that work, though difficult, must be done in order to live well; children do what's *pleasing*, always trying to evade the difficult or uncomfortable. Just check out a child's response to any assigned work, to any routine chore. Students of psychology speak of "infantile self-gratification." I just call it laziness. Children naturally tend to be lazy, to lie around watching TV rather than cleaning the bathroom.

Making fun life's goal veils the sorrow of not doing anything substantial, and when we're too young to be able to do much, there's little inner satisfaction. So we naturally, quite normally, seek to have fun. What we really need, what we deeply long for, is to know we are in fact competent, able to do good things well.

That, incidentally, is why children need, more than most anything other than love, daily chores. No healthy kid *wants* to do chores, but kids *need* them more than they know. One of the ultimate cruelties parents lay on their kids is to let them play all day, every day. For it's only when we learn the value of routine and worthwhile work that we begin to understand and appreciate the fuller joys of creativity.

Real joy, genuine satisfaction, we find, comes from *doing* something substantial. Being amused, wanting to have fun, leaves us empty, lacking substance. But giving ourselves to something, expending our energies, concretely accomplishing something lifts us up, gives us a zest for life. It isn't always pleasant, but it's worthwhile.

Jesus calls us to be disciples, to take the road less traveled, because "he knows that his mission is a rugged minority movement," says Dale Bruner, "a tough, divisive affair, and he prefers to make this clear rather than give false hope."[14]

I've been thinking about the fact that though Jesus loved children, though He said, "Suffer the little children to come unto me, and forbid them not: for of such is the kingdom of God" (Mark 10:14, KJV), He never opened a Sunday School. He didn't gather a group of kids for a backyard Bible study. He seemed uninterested in youth ministry. He sought out young men, but they were *mature* young men who could do the work of living and proclaiming His gospel.

Discipline Determines Destinies

Consequently, these young men belonged to "the company of the committed," to use the title of one of Elton Trueblood's books. They who follow Jesus find family ties in the family of God more precious than in any human family. In Matt. 12:46-50, we read:

> While Jesus was still talking to the crowd, his mother and brothers stood outside, wanting to speak to him. Someone told him, "Your mother and brothers are standing outside, wanting to speak to you."
>
> He replied to him, "Who is my mother, and who are my brothers?" Pointing to his disciples, he said, "Here are my mother and my brothers. For whoever does the will of my Father in heaven is my brother and sister and mother."

Clearly, Jesus calls us to make decisions, disciplined decisions, that characterize disciples, and it's disciples who join Jesus in living out the way of life God has designed for us.

A century ago Dwight L. Moody preached a series of messages for a group of college students at a retreat center in Mount Hermon, near Northfield, Massachusetts. Also present was a missionary who urged young people to re spond to the challenge of world missions. At the end of the retreat, exactly 100 young collegians committed themselves to full-time missionary service. In a few months they returned to their colleges and shared the joy of their decision. In a brief period of time some 5,000 young Americans, the corps of the Student Volunteer Movement, the best and brightest of their generation, gave themselves to spreading the good news of Jesus throughout the world. As a result of their courage and work, today there are growing Christian churches in places such as Korea, China, and Africa. They made a difference, an eternal difference, in the lives of millions of people. They made critical decisions.[15]

Decisions demand discipline, and discipline determines destinies. And our ultimate obedience is to our Heavenly Father, our ultimate allegiance to His kingdom, rather than our biological families.

8

The Sanctity of Life

OLD TESTAMENT FOUNDATION: DO NOT MURDER

One of the stars of the United States' 1992 Olympic basketball "dream team," Charles Barkley, in talking to a reporter in Barcelona during the games, insisted that Spain was nice but that he really missed the U.S.A.

"I miss America," he said. "I miss crime and murder. I miss Philadelphia. There hasn't been a brutal stabbing or anything here in the last 24 hours. I've missed it."

There's heavy irony in Barkley's words, of course. Lots of us love America, but our land is awash with bloodshed.

In America since 1900 some 10,000 people a year have been murdered—a century's total of a million or so. Babies born in the 1970s were more likely to be murdered than American soldiers killed in World War II. In America young males are 20 times as likely to be murdered as their European counterparts, 40 times as likely as their Japanese peers. Folks kill folks.

And they always have, long before America was settled. If you're interested in gory details, the historical record provides them. Centuries ago a Hungarian countess, Erszebet Bathory (1560-1614), was accused of killing 610 young girls, the names of whom she carefully recorded in her notebook. A bit earlier a Chinese named Chang

Hsien-Chung seized control of the province of Szechwan, where in five years he killed 40 million people, including 280 of his own wives! We are, it seems, born killers.

Whether we study the newspapers, history books, or our own experiences, we should conclude that our society is violent because we (you and I) are by nature capable of violence. Like an automobile's tempered spring, we're inflexibly bent toward it. At all times, in all places, earth has been dyed red with blood. Day after day, year after year, the killing goes on.

How long will it take, we wonder, to stop the killing? How long will we go on murdering our brothers and sisters, fathers and sons? Quite frankly, unlike the utopians who advertise their fantasies on bumper stickers, urging us to "visualize world peace," we'll never abolish violence. It's simply a part of the crimson bent toward evil ingrained in our sinful nature. Despite that, the Bible calls us who want to live with God into a covenant relationship with Him, which makes it clear, in the words of the sixth commandment, "You shall not murder" (Exod. 20:13).

The Crime Defined: An Anatomy of Murder

The Hebrew word used in this passage (Exod. 20:13) appears only 40 times in the Old Testament. It clearly condemns deliberately taking an innocent person's life—what the law labels murder. Other words are used for "killing" or causing death, such as what happens in self-defense, police action, or just war.

What concerns us here is that "innocent blood will not be shed" (Deut. 19:10). With this in mind, at least five kinds of killing—the deliberate taking of innocent life—are forbidden: premeditated murder, abortion, mercy killing, unjust war, and suicide. Let's consider only two of these life-and-death issues: premeditated murder and abortion.

Most clearly, the Scripture condemns first-degree, premeditated murder. To study an anatomy of a murder, turn to the beginning of human history, recorded in Genesis, where we read the story of Cain killing Abel. The first step in the making of a murderer begins when Cain turns away from God. The text doesn't indicate the precise problem, but it's evident that Cain wanted to do things his way rather than God's.

Abel offered God his best, but Cain seems to have grabbed a couple of apples and a handful of wheat and insisted that God accept whatever he presented. It's like a man who has asked a woman to a fancy banquet (where all the women will wear nice corsages) and picks some dandelions and eucalyptus leaves, ties them together with a shoestring, and expects her to be impressed with his gift.

So it is with many alleged believers. Lots of folks claim to be "born again," but not all of them want to give God what He wants. They want His blessings but not His directions.

Consider the story of George Taylor. As a youngster he got in trouble and spent four years in a Michigan prison. Resolving to stay out of trouble, when he got out he went to a Bible college and took some courses at Fuller Theological Seminary. Then he pastored a church and built it into a congregation of 800.

But he wanted to be a millionaire, so he cut the wrong corners and ended up back in prison. As he diagnosed it, "I still wasn't totally committed. I wore the label 'Christian' just like a lot of folks. I don't question what a person says he is, but you have to look at his lifestyle—can you see a clear-cut value system?" That's what he discovered in prison, especially when he had a long talk with Chuck Colson—the first person Taylor had met who had truly surrendered everything to follow Jesus.

Impressed by Colson's integrity, Taylor totally yielded himself to Christ. He now calls himself a "junkman." "I've come off the junk pile," he says. "I don't forget from whence I've come, but somebody laundered me. When you get cleaned up from inside out, you don't just believe it—you live it."[1]

Cain refused to live it. He stepped away from the Lord, and the next step led him to shift his focus to himself and his own interests, languishing in self-pity because the Lord failed to accept his substitute offering. Hardly anything is more pathetic than a "pity party." But lots of us regularly throw them! Cain pouted. His face was "downcast" with a "pout cloud."

Here I can identify with Cain. I've never been one to scream and throw things, but I really know how to get stone-cold quiet and sullen, to pout like a pro. When I was young, my dad made me work with him on various projects—tearing down houses, building houses, working on cars, mowing the lawn. Dad seemed to think there was nothing more fun than work, and he didn't want me to miss out on the fun. I, on the other hand, thought my healthy development as a child depended upon more time spent playing football with my friends or (when we finally got a set) watching TV. Strangely enough, however, Dad's interests always prevailed, and I worked a lot—something I'm now grateful for.

I remember that while I was working, I would be occasionally nearly overwhelmed with sullen self-pity. In those moments I actually fantasized that it would just serve my dad right if I would collapse and die from overwork. I didn't want to die, but I did want folks to pity me. Then the whole world would know what a mean dad I had and how I suffered under his mistreatment. Before it became popular to celebrate one's "victimhood" status, I discovered its self-righteous feelings.

Cain first turned away from God, then turned to pitying himself and pouting. In that condition he opened his mind and heart to sin. The Scripture reads: "Then the LORD said to Cain, 'Why are you angry? Why is your face down-cast? If you do what is right, will you not be accepted? But if you do not do what is right, sin is crouching at your door; it desires to have you, but you must master it" (Gen. 4:6-7).

Cain chose to do wrong. Having turned away from God, having turned his attention to himself and his griev-ance, he then turned against his brother. He crafted a plan. He envisioned a way to entice, entrap, and eliminate his brother. He *premeditated* murder. Perhaps he said, "Hey, brother Abel—the trout are biting in the stream. Let's go catch some." Whatever the ruse, as soon as they were alone, "Cain attacked his brother Abel and killed him" (v. 8). He turned on his brother with evil intent. Perhaps he used a rock or a spear. Who knows? He killed.

The deed done, Cain next switched off his conscience. He evaded God's question, "Where is your brother Abel?" (v. 9).

"How should I know?" he seemed to say. "Am I my brother's keeper?" (v. 9). Perhaps he tried to lie, saying, "Abel's probably playing in the fields, practicing his spear throwing. Why, he's so reckless he may spear himself one of these days." But the truth was that Cain had murdered Abel and couldn't evade God's judgment.

Included in the prohibition of first-degree murder, we today face the plague of abortion, the killing of over a million unborn American children each year, a tragedy John Powell calls "the silent holocaust." It's something that po-larizes people, one of the major battlegrounds in the "cul-ture wars," and neither side seems about to abandon its stance. So it's important to discern and champion the truth as cogently as possible.

Francis J. Beckwith, a lecturer in philosophy at the University of Nevada, Las Vegas, provides us with one of the finest antiabortion treatises available: *Politically Correct Death: Answering Arguments for Abortion Rights*.[2] Part of the book's strength is the logician's care with which Beckwith defines terms, using the more accurate label "abortion rights" to designate the "pro-choice" position.

Beckwith explains why abortion on demand is legal in America, meticulously explaining the contents of important Supreme Court decisions. He then shows why, as a result, "it is safe to say that in the first six months of pregnancy a woman can have an abortion for no reason, but in the last three months she can have it for any reason. This is abortion on demand."[3]

To construct a case against it, Beckwith summarizes the most recent data concerning prenatal development, generally arguing, with Dr. Seuss, that "a person is a person, no matter how small."[4] At the moment of conception, a radically different organism comes into being. The "zygote," a one-celled entity, cannot be called a "fertilized ovum," because "both ovum and sperm, which are genetically each a part of its owner (mother and father, respectively), cease to exist at the moment of conception."[5]

The simple fact that a genetically Asian test-tube baby, conceived in a petri dish, would be clearly Asian at birth, even if implanted and nurtured in the surrogate womb of a Swedish woman, shows that the "conceptus is *not* part of the woman's body."[6] In truth, few abortion-rights statements are more demonstrably false than the oft-quoted refrain that "a woman has a right to do whatever she wants with her own body." Abortion does not excise "tissue" from a woman—it ends the life of an unborn child who resides in the womb.

Many abortion-rights arguments follow a 1920 statement by the founder of Planned Parenthood, Margaret Sanger: "The most merciful thing a large family can do for one of its infant members is to kill it."[7] Pity the poor child so as to free him from poverty's pains by killing him! Basically, such arguments fail to address the real issue: Is what is killed in abortion in fact human? If so, our "pity" for the pregnant woman facing difficulties should not move us to kill the child. We may pity the poor man who steals, but we rarely approve his theft—especially if he steals from *us!*

Though the Bible says little about abortion per se, the Early Church adamantly opposed it.[8] The world into which Christianity came easily tolerated abortion. A society that allowed infanticide could not be overly exercised by abortions. The satirist Juvenal noted that Rome's wealthy women rarely got pregnant, because money allowed them to purchase abortions. Some women apparently wanted to maintain their trim appearance and sought to avoid the swollen stomach and restricted activities pregnancy involves.[9]

The Hippocratic oath, of course, called on physicians to "not give to a woman a pessary to cause abortion,"[10] and some of the great natural law thinkers, such as Cicero, opposed abortion. Alone among ancient peoples, the Jews strongly condemned the practice. Though the Hebrew Scriptures did not clearly address it, by and large the Jews did not practice abortion. The only item at issue that divided the rabbis concerned the penalty necessary when *"accidental or therapeutic* abortion" occurred.

Early Christians sided with the pro-life Stoics and Jews. The New Testament doesn't specifically mention abortion, but second-century documents (the *Didache* and the *Epistle of Barnabas*) directly denounce it. It was considered a form of murder, forbidden by the Law. Athenagoras wrote: "We say that women who induce abortions are murderers."[11] Early councils and the most influential of the church fathers (Tertullian, Origen, Basil of Caesarea, Ambrose, Augustine, John Chrysostom, Jerome) all adamantly condemned it. As penance, church members who aborted a child were often barred from Communion for 10 years. It was clearly considered one of the gravest of all sins.

Though the ancient world is long gone, the issue is utterly contemporary. As paganism, resurfacing like graffiti on overpasses, establishes its values, abortion becomes more acceptable. But if the Church today is to follow the example of the Church of antiquity—the Church of the martyrs and saints—its position on abortion will likely be one of the indicators of its fidelity and integrity.

Covenant Commitment: Revere Life

There are many ramifications to the prohibition "Thou shalt not kill" (Exod. 20:13, KJV). But more important for the people of God is the positive proposition underlying the commandment: living with the Lord of life enables us to rejoice in the beauty of life and to join God in preserving it. Underlying the prohibition is an injunction: celebrate the sanctity of life, for human life is even more than sacred—it's *sacrosanct*, precious because it's God's gift to us.

That ancient reverence for human life, rooted in the very will of God, stands revealed in God's covenant with Noah immediately after the Flood. It's recorded in one of the most illuminating passages in God's Word: "And from each man, too, I will demand an accounting for the life of his fellow man. Whoever sheds the blood of man, by man shall his blood be shed; for in the image of God has God made man" (Gen. 9:5-6).

Then God sketched a rainbow in the sky, an eternally recurring sign of His covenant, binding himself to us and all living creatures. Life's a gift, *sacrosanct*, and we must treasure it. In the words of an African proverb, "Human blood is heavy; the man who has shed it cannot run away."

Gifts are important. Years ago I spoke for a Native American youth camp. At the end of the week a Comanche friend gave me a ring as a token of friendship. It was too big for me, and when I got home, my wife asked what I planned to do with the ring. She suggested she might like to wear it on a chain as a necklace, so I gave it to her.

The next year, somewhat unexpectedly, I spoke for the same camp. When I met my friend Mike, he asked, "Where's your ring?" (I confess I really wanted to lie a little at that point!) I told him the truth: I'd given it to my wife. He then informed me that if I wanted to give my wife a ring, I should *buy* one from him for her. He had given me the ring as an act of friendship. I agreed. I ordered a ring for her and paid Mike for it. Then I went home, took back my ring, had it reduced to fit my finger, and now treasure it as a reminder of a generous act. It's a gift worth preserving.

Even more important, we've been given a gift of life, a precious gift from the Lord and Giver of life. I deeply appreciate the gift. So do you! So I urge you to join me, to join the Lord above, and treasure the gift of life—upholding God's covenant with Noah, inscribed in the sixth commandment, refusing to take from others what God has given them.

NEW TESTAMENT INTERNALIZATION: NURSE NO ANGER

Do you ever wonder about the amount of anger that seethes like a pressure cooker all around us? There's lots of anger surging across our land. It's an anger that often looks as if it could kill. And if looks could kill, there'd be lots of dead bodies littering the land!

There's anger etched into the faces of various protesters—I'm amazed by the hateful expressions on both abortion-rights and antiabortion advocates as they march in the streets, shouting and even hurling things to vent their convictions. There's anger inscribed in the lyrics of rock musicians, rap musicians, singers who venomously attack a world they apparently find hostile.

There's anger in our communities. A few years ago I was walking along a street near my home and saw an elderly man chasing a handful of junior high boys who were on roller blades. He had a steel rod in his hand and hurled it at them. It missed and clattered down the street. Then one of the boys picked up the rod and took off after the man, who hustled back up the street. The boy tossed the rod and also missed. Then the man and his wife came back toward the boys. At that point I intervened (fools rush in where angels fear to tread, I guess) and tried to cool things down. Mainly I tried to talk with the boys, who seemed to be the antagonists in the altercation, but I did little more than give both sides time to cool down. It seems the boys played pranks and had otherwise irritated the elderly couple. Finally the man got so mad he resorted to rod throwing. That's dangerous! It even bordered on the ridiculous. But it illustrates how anger gets explosive.

Is there any solution? We can pass laws to punish murder, but we have no way to wash out the anger that wells up in the hearts of murderers. In fact, there's only one solution I know: the Jesus solution. Jesus said, deepening the Old Testament's prohibition of murder, "You have heard that it was said to the people long ago, 'Do not murder, and anyone who murders will be subject to judgment.' But I tell you that anyone who is angry with his brother will be subject to judgment" (Matt. 5:21-22).

Nurse No Grudges! Renounce Revenge!

Rooted in Jesus' statement, Christian thinkers have identified anger as one of the seven deadly sins, one of the sins that surely separates us from God. It's important to understand that the anger condemned is not a passing emotion, not a hurt feeling, but *nursing the will for revenge,* nursing a grudge.

There are two Greek words for "anger." One, *thumos,* describes the rapid, explosive emotion that responds to injury or injustice.

When someone sticks a knife into your back, you bleed.

That's a normal, healthy reaction to the injury. When someone attacks us, physically or verbally, we feel anger. That's a normal, healthy reaction to assault. We might prefer not to bleed, we might be embarrassed by the bloody mess we make, but we'll bleed. If someone hits me in the solar plexus, I'll probably not say, "Oh, wow, thanks—I needed that. Kinda makes my day." No, I'll feel *thumos*, anger.

The other kind of anger, *orgē*, means a lasting, furious, vengeful desire to see an enemy suffer. Though the phrase "without a cause" (Matt. 5:22, KJV) is not found in the best Greek manuscripts, both John Chrysostom and Augustine, who were preaching at the end of the fourth century, used versions that included the clause, for it seemed to them the anger Jesus condemned needed to be clearly understood as a will to vengeance rather than an emotional reaction. As F. Dale Bruner says in his fine commentary on Matthew, the Greek phrase "literally means 'is *being* angry,' 'bears anger,' 'carries anger,' or in our idiom, 'nurses a grudge.'"[12]

This kind of anger, *orgē*, is succinctly phrased in the motto some folks live by: "Don't get angry—get even." A prominent Spanish general and statesman, Ramón María Narváez, lay dying in 1869. A priest asked him: "Does Your Excellency forgive all your enemies?" Replied Narváez: "I do not have to forgive my enemies. I have had them all shot."[13] Now that's a graphic way to get even.

But it is, in fact, difficult if not impossible to get even. We usually do more harm to ourselves than to our enemies when we try to right the scales of justice. Consider the case of a woman who came to Ibn Sa'ūd, the first king of Saudi Arabia, in 1932. She approached the king, seeking to have the man who had killed her husband executed.

It seems the accused man had been gathering dates in a palm tree, slipped, and fell on her husband, fatally injuring him. So the king asked if the fall had been deliberate. Were the two men enemies? Apparently they didn't know each other, and the fall was purely accidental. But the widow demanded revenge: life for life.

Ibn Sa'ūd tried to reason with her, urging her to accept a cash settlement or something else. But she demanded a life for a life. Finally the king relented. He said: "It is your right to exact compensation, and it is also your right to ask for this man's life. But it is my right to decree how he shall die. You shall take this man with you, and he shall be tied to the foot of a palm tree, and then you yourself shall climb to the top of the tree and cast yourself down upon him from that height. In that way you will take his life as he took your husband's."

There was a long pause. "Or perhaps," Ibn Sa'ūd added, "you would prefer after all to take the blood money?" The widow wisely took the money.[14]

Call No One "Stupid"! Avoid Put-downs!

Having warned against nursing a grudge, Jesus continued: "Again, anyone who says to his brother, 'Raca,' is answerable to the Sanhedrin" (v. 22). Not only are we to forsake revenge, but also we're to avoid lashing out at people, calling them names, saying things like "Raca," which means "You idiot," "Stupid," "Dum-dum." How often we say, with words and looks and intonations, "Oh, you stupid you!" That's *raca*. For *raca* reflects contempt for another person, the attitude that he or she is somehow second-class, unworthy of respect.

We say, "Raca," more by the tone of our voice, the looks that accompany our speech, than by code words of some sort. Now and then my wife rebukes me (reminding me how clearly we communicate without words) by saying, "You're giving me that 'Oh, you stupid you' look." One of my friends once applied a biblical phrase to me, saying, "Gerard doesn't 'suffer fools gladly.'" And I took it as a rebuke, not a compliment. I need to know I have the tendency, the ability, to put down folks who are not on my wavelength, who fail to measure up to whatever standard I'm using.

When King James I ruled England, a less-than-notable envoy appeared in court. Later the king asked Francis Bacon what he thought of the marquis.

"Your Majesty," Bacon said, "people of such dimensions are like four- or five-story houses—the upper rooms are the most poorly furnished."[15]

So we say, "She's an airhead," or "He's not running on all cylinders," or "He's carrying something less than a full load."

And we easily make intellectual distinctions. In the academic world where I live, Ph.D.'s look down on Ed.D.'s. Ph.D.'s and Ed.D.'s make fun of D.D.'s. There's too often an incredible arrogance in intellectuals, who easily divide the world into the smart folks and the dumb folks. We teachers, I think, must struggle continually to avoid labeling young people "bright" or "dull" simply because of the grades they get in our classes—or the scores they make on S.A.T. tests—or the I.Q. labels with which they're branded.

A psychologist at Harvard University recently insisted that there are at least seven distinct kinds of intelligence. In school we measure only two: mathematical and verbal. The kind of intelligence needed in music, art, interpersonal relationships, and athletics is not easily identified and certainly is not much measured in school. I'm sure athletes are weary of "dumb jock" jokes. I can admit to being musically inept or athletically slow and still be judged intelligent, since I have verbal skills. But musicians and athletes must also excel in math and English to be considered "smart." Not so!

Call No One "Fool"! Cease Condemning
Still more: Jesus said, "Anyone who says, 'You fool!' will be in danger of the fire of hell" (v. 22). Whereas "raca" means "stupid," the word "fool" refers to a person's moral character. We call a man a "fool" when we malign his good

name, when we destroy his reputation as a person of moral integrity. To call a person a "scoundrel," to label a person a "no-good," is to seek to take God's place in judging—and damning—persons. We're told to "judge not, that ye be not judged" (7:1, KJV).

Over a century ago Henry Ward Beecher was one of the most prominent men in America. Weekly he preached to thousands in New York City's Plymouth Church. One Sunday he arrived and found a letter to him containing one word: FOOL. He told the people about it that day, adding: "I have known many an instance of a man writing a letter and forgetting to sign his name, but this is the only instance I have ever known of a man signing his name and forgetting to write the letter."[16] Would that all of us could respond to criticism and condemnation with Beecher's humor. But even humor cannot undo the harm done by harsh words, critical comments, and malicious gossip.

Certainly we are languaging creatures. We use words —some of us use them incessantly. Jesus said there are folks with eyes who see not and folks with ears who hear not. He never said there are folks with tongues that speak not. We certainly keep our mouths in motion. Lots of us are, to tell the truth, motormouths. And many of our tongues seem to run fastest when our brains are idling. Perhaps speaking for lots of old-timers, an elderly man said, "Many of us are like a pair of old shoes—all worn out but the tongue." In my observation, tongues rarely wear out.

The Jewish Talmud tells of a king who sent two of his court jesters on a mission. "Foolish Simon," the king said, "go and bring back the best thing in the world. And you, Silly John, go and find me the worst thing in the world." Both jesters quickly departed and almost as quickly returned with a package. Simon bowed before the king, saying, "Behold, Sire, the best thing in the world." His package contained a human tongue. Silly John then snickered and undid his package, saying, "The worst thing in the world, Sire!" Another human tongue!

So we've been given the best—and the worst—thing in the world: a tongue. The question today for me is this—how will I use it? To walk with Jesus, to talk as Jesus talks, means to let His love, present in the power of His Holy Spirit, free us from resentment and deliver us from the temptation to use our tongues as weapons of destruction. When we think about controlling the tongue, it seems humanly impossible. And it is. Only the new covenant, whereby God has promised to put His law in our hearts, enables us to speak in a Christlike manner.

When we think about what Jesus says, most of us are driven to despair of ever doing what He urges. How can anyone live like this? That's precisely what He wants us to discover. On our own we never will. Immediately before this passage, He said that "unless your righteousness surpasses that of the Pharisees and the teachers of the law, you will certainly not enter the kingdom of heaven" (5:20).

So how are we to get in? Only by His gracious assistance. To live as Jesus wants us to, we must learn, as did Brother Lawrence, that "When an occasion of practicing some virtue was offered, he addressed himself to God, saying, *Lord, I cannot do this unless thou enablest me;* and that then he received strength more than sufficient."

9

The Sanctity of Sex

OLD TESTAMENT FOUNDATION: ADULTERY? NO!

"Jack and Elaine Kirschke were nothing if not adult about adultery," began a *Time* magazine article years ago. "He liked women and she liked men, and neither was a spoilsport. There was only one house rule for their not-quite-home on voguish Rivo Alto Canal in Naples, California: when one party had the pad, the other stayed away."[1]

Married for 24 years, both were prosperous professionals (she a fashion designer, he a chief prosecutor for the Los Angeles district attorney), good-looking, and "cool." They had it all together—until Jack killed Elaine and her latest lover. Sometimes we're not as "adult about adultery" as we pretend.

But we certainly keep on doing it. In *The Day America Told the Truth*, one chapter is titled "Infidelity: It's Rampant."[2] Almost one-third of married Americans have had or are having affairs. According to researchers Peter Kim and James Patterson, "The majority of Americans (62 percent) think that there's nothing morally wrong with the affairs they're having. Once again, we hear the killer rationalization that 'everybody does it too.'" Interestingly enough, however, these adulterers themselves do not think their spouses are the "everybodies" doing it.[3] Somehow spouses of adulterers are supposed to be faithful to their unfaithful partners.

These are recent illustrations, but actually adultery is as old as the human race. With some justification prostitution has been called "the oldest profession," for if human sinfulness is evident anywhere, it's in our disordered sexual conduct—to which the Scripture simply says, in the words of the seventh commandment, "You shall not commit adultery" (Exod. 20:14). This commandment, like the others, is easy to understand. It is, however, as history reveals, terribly difficult to follow.

One teacher in a religion class, asking her students to recite the Ten Commandments, was taken aback when one of them remembered the first six flawlessly, then said: "Thou shalt not admit adultery." He'd captured the mood of modernity. It's clearly the policy of many celebrities—politicians, singers, televangelists. One father, responding to his young son's question concerning a Sunday School lesson on the Ten Commandments, was amused when the lad asked what the Bible meant by saying, "Thou shalt not commit agriculture." Wisely, Dad responded, "That means you're not to plow in your neighbor's field." Sure enough. Stay true to your own mate.

Infidelity Is Always a Threat

To grasp the importance of this commandment, consider these words in the Book of Proverbs that illustrate why Proverbs condemns adultery:

> For the lips of an adulteress drip honey,
>   and her speech is smoother than oil;
> but in the end she is bitter as gall,
>   sharp as a double-edged sword.
> Her feet go down to death;
>   her steps lead straight to the grave.
> She gives no thought to the way of life;
>   her paths are crooked, but she knows it not.
>   (5:3-6)

Our world is full of temptations. We struggle daily with them. While they come in diverse forms, the world abounds with sexual tempters and temptresses. Too many folks live by the Zsa Zsa rule. Zsa Zsa Gabor, as you know, is the oft married Hollywood film star. A magazine writer once asked her, as well as some other prominent women, "What is the first thing you notice about a woman?"

"Her way of speaking," was mystery writer Agatha Christie's answer.

"Her hands," said Maria Callas, the opera singer.

With unusual candor, Zsa Zsa declared: "Her husband."[4] Whether true or not, such stories illustrate the "Hollywood ethos" that thoroughly pervades our society.

The text in Proverbs continues, giving advice that is as relevant to us as to ancient Israel:

> Now then, my sons, listen to me;
>   do not turn aside from what I say.
> Keep to a path far from her,
>   do not go near the door of her house,
> lest you give your best strength to others
>   and your years to one who is cruel,
> lest strangers feast on your wealth
>   and your toil enrich another man's house.
> At the end of your life you will groan,
>   when your flesh and body are spent.
> You will say, "How I hated discipline!
>   How my heart spurned correction!
> I would not obey my teachers
>   or listen to my instructors.
> I have come to the brink of utter ruin
>   in the midst of the whole assembly."
>
> *(5:7-14)*

Temptations, when embraced, bring (in the long run) little but grief and sorrow. In the short run they're exciting, but in the long run they're as devastating as a Mississippi flood. Adultery is so insidious because it so easily destroys what's most precious. If I were to bring $1 million into a room and begin burning the money, folks nearby would protest. It's just wrong to waste something that's precious. If I brought Leonardo's *Mona Lisa* into a shopping mall and started shredding it with a knife, I imagine someone would physically restrain me. It's demonstrably wrong to destroy a precious work of art. Similarly, marriage is precious, and it's wrong to destroy it.

Yet millions of folks argue that it's fine to sleep around. Of course, they say it's acceptable only as long as the folks involved are "consenting adults," as long as "no one gets hurt." Whatever their married estate, there's nothing to worry about as long as everyone involved gets some satisfaction, they say.

But let me argue that someone always gets hurt. Whenever I donate blood at the blood bank, I'm reminded, as I answer the seemingly endless questions about my sexual contacts, that folks who need blood need *good* blood. I'm reminded of the thousands of innocent hemophiliacs who are dying because their blood transfusions were tainted with the AIDS virus. Some folks claim to think monogamy is obsolete, unnecessary, irrelevant. But they'll not be welcome at the blood bank.

Good blood comes from right living. Good marriages come with right living as well. Even more: keeping marriage vows builds spiritual integrity. The integrity we inwardly hunger for comes with sustained commitment to a lasting, loving relationship with our spouse. Adultery, in Scripture, means infidelity to one's husband or wife. What's wrong with adultery is not merely the pleasure of promiscuous sex—it's the breaking of vows, the breaking of solemn promises. It's forbidden because we're called to be promise keepers, covenant-keeping people. Keeping promises keeps us human. Few things more clearly mark a fundamentally good person than his or her faithfulness.

Marriage Matters, for Vows Validate Integrity

The spirituality of sex can be sustained only within long-term monogamous relationships. Since adultery annihilates such relationships, the Bible insists that we not commit adultery. For not only does adultery disrupt human bonds—but it distances us from God. In committing adultery, we turn away from Yahweh, rejecting His Lordship over all realms of existence.

Returning to our text in Prov. 5:

> Drink water from your own cistern,
>   running water from your own well.
> Should your springs overflow in the streets,
>   your streams of water in the public squares?
> Let them be yours alone,
>   never to be shared with strangers.
> May your fountain be blessed,
>   and may you rejoice in the wife of your youth.
> A loving doe, a graceful deer—
>   may her breasts satisfy you always,
>   may you ever be captivated by her love.
> Why be captivated, my son, by an adulteress?
>   Why embrace the bosom of another man's wife?
>
> *(vv. 15-20)*

Fidelity! Faithfulness! Nothing means more to a person than staying true to the vows he or she has made to a person. I read that the now permanently separated Princess Diana and Prince Charles of England began to have difficulties with their marriage on their honeymoon. It seems the prince actually wore a ring, composed of two strands of interwoven gold, that had been given him by one of his former flames. How cruel! How difficult it would be for any woman—Princess Di included—to know her husband still cherished someone other than her.

If you study English history, you know the royal family has had its share of philanderers. In 1910 King Edward VII died. He was a notorious adulterer, forcing his wife, Alexandra, a Danish princess, to pretend she didn't see what all the world knew. When her husband died, Alexandra was momentarily grief-stricken, but then she brightened up and, with a sense of humor, said, "Now at least I know where he is."

Well, the Bible calls us to a better way. Thus, the guiding assumption of the Old Testament is this: sex and marriage are good when they're kept sacred by fidelity.

Years ago Alex Comfort published a best-seller titled *The Joy of Sex*, which was basically a how-to-do-it manual. The book might better have been titled "The Pleasures of Sex." But Comfort picked the right title, for there's a deep joy to a lasting sexual bond that helps unite persons who deeply love one another.

We're not to commit adultery, because marriage can be so good. There's nothing sweeter than sex in marriage. There's nothing better than drinking "water from your own cistern," rejoicing "in the wife of your youth." Some of our grandparents, some of our great-grandparents have been married for decades. If we want to know something about the "joy of sex," we'd be wise to follow their example rather than that of the Hollywood stars who yearly jump from bed to bed, apparently in quest of elusive pleasures, of fresh "fun" times.

There is, in fact, a joy to sex that transcends its fun. The joy of sex comes when two persons trust each other enough to enjoy the real intimacy that comes from living together, sharing life together. It's what Martin Luther wisely described when he said, "Let the wife make her husband glad to come home, and let him make her sorry to see him leave."

This truth gains documentation in a recent work by Andrew Greeley, *Faithful Attraction: Discovering Intimacy, Love, and Fidelity in American Marriage.*[5] He draws on the most trustworthy of recent public opinion polls to validate the soundness of marriage in America, insisting that "fidelity is common in American marriage."[6] Rather than relying on impressionistic, anecdotal, journalistic accounts or skewed polls like the oft-cited (and notoriously flawed) *Kinsey Report* or *Hite Reports,* Greeley grounds this study in a 1989-90 Gallup poll, "the first full-scale national probability sample study of sexuality and fidelity in marriage" plus another equally careful research project.[7] To the extent we can find accurate sociological data regarding the subject, Greeley provides it.

Given the largely negative press about marriage and family (evident in a 1987 *Newsweek* cover story that prodded Greeley's study), this work provides a healthy, encouraging antidote. For he argues—and provides the data needed—that marriages in this country remain solidly monogamous and strong (especially where religious faith exists) and provide couples maximal happiness.

Throughout the various items viewed, one factor emerges: religion improves marriage. It's the most important common denominator in strong marriages, and "there is no stronger predictor of marital happiness than religious devotion."[8] Spouses who share religious convictions "are 27 percentage points more likely to report agreement on general values," and, even more impressive, the percentage rises to 36 if they go to church each week.[9] Only 11 percent of those who pray together think divorce might be possible, compared to 30 percent of those who don't.

Still more: "Only 1 percent of those who pray together often and report the highest quality of sex think divorce is possible."[10] "God and pleasure are, quite literally, a hard combination to beat."[11] Nearly one-third of the respondents regularly pray with their spouse. "Whether they pray often together or not is a very powerful correlate of marital happiness, the most powerful we have yet discovered. Seventy-five percent of those who pray say that the marriage is very happy, as opposed to 57 percent of those who do not pray so often."[12] Indeed, "Prayer, it is worth noting [better predicts] . . . marital satisfaction than frequency of sexual intercourse—though the combination of sex and prayer correlates with very, very high levels of marital fulfillment."[13]

Despite the generally upbeat tone of this tome, there are some discouraging words. Divorce continues to rip apart marriages and families; one in every two of today's marriages seems destined to dissolve. Divorce leaves women, especially, impoverished and disadvantaged. In almost requiring that women work, modern society has placed considerable strain on those who try to sustain both marriage and vocation. Greeley's study shows that today's working women are less happy than housewives of an earlier generation—but they are not less happy with marriage. What distresses them is a society that demands they work full-time as career women and still be full-time mothers.

Though there are certainly problems in the contemporary home, this book provides substantial reasons, especially for Christians, to face the future with confidence. Marriage and the family have survived and will survive. And it's nice to have some data to fuel our hopes.

NEW TESTAMENT INTERNALIZATION: CHASTITY? YES!

Many of us would like to be Christians; indeed, many of us readily identify ourselves as Christians. In fact, a 1992 survey revealed 80 percent of the American populace claim to be "Christian."

But we're not too sure what that means. There are lots of diverse definitions. Some have simply said yes to a presentation of the "Four Spiritual Laws." Others have joined a church. Some remember a special feeling, an exhilarating experience years ago.

Let me argue that to be a Christian means living a life that pleases God, a life sanctified by God's Spirit, who enables us truly to love God. To all who want to *be* Christian, let me remind you of the wisdom of the ancient Church. In the early centuries, the best thinkers of the Church set forth the "evangelical counsels," some ways of pursuing spiritual perfection: chastity, simplicity, humility. Clearly rooted in Jesus' wilderness temptations, they find concise expression in the words of the "Beloved Disciple," John, who said:

> Love not the world, neither the things that are in the world. If any man love the world, the love of the Father is not in him. For all that is in the world, the lust of the flesh, and the lust of the eyes, and the pride of life, is not of the Father, but is of the world. And the world passeth away, and the lust thereof: but he that doeth the will of God abideth for ever *(1 John 2:15-17, KJV)*.

To live with God means to handle sex, money, and power rightly. Right now let's consider sex, using a passage from 1 Thessalonians as our guide. This is probably Paul's first letter, written from Corinth in A.D. 51. He had just been in Thessalonica and wrote to remind the young church of the basics of the Christian faith. In the first three chapters he stressed doctrinal essentials. In the fourth chapter he turns practical, telling them "how to live in order to please God" (v. 1).

> It is God's will that you should be sanctified: that you should avoid sexual immorality; that each of you should learn to control his own body in a way that is holy and honorable, not in passionate lust like the heathen, who do not know God; and that in this matter no one should wrong his brother or take advantage of him. The Lord will punish men for all such sins, as we have already told you and warned you. For God did not call us to be impure, but to live a holy life *(vv. 3-7)*.

Abstain from Fornication!

To follow the Holy Spirit's direction, according to the above text, means we "avoid sexual immorality," that we "abstain from fornication" (v. 3, KJV). There's a sexual dimension to sanctification, a sexual tone to the good life.

One of the main themes that unites all of Scripture is *faithfulness to the covenant.* As a central theme in the Bible, faithfulness is best illustrated in marriage, the paradigm of promise keeping.

In Albert Camus's *The Fall,* an insightful atheist lamented, "I sometimes think of what future historians will say of us. A single sentence will suffice for modern man: he fornicated and read the papers."[14]

That pretty much sums it up! Modernity celebrates sexuality and propaganda. In response, Christians need to bear witness to their faith by refusing to accept the modern mood. Simply saying no to illicit sex—fornication, impure behavior—is part of the Christian ethos. Paul wrote to believers surrounded by sexual promiscuity, a world much like modern America, and they needed to know why to say no to fornication. Eunice Kennedy Shriver says:

> Recently, I went to a center for teenage girls where the teacher asked what they would like to discuss most. Human biology? Care for their infant? Physiology of childbirth? Family planning? The girls showed no interest. Then the teacher asked, "Would you like to discuss how to say no to your boyfriend without losing his love?" All hands shot up.[15]

For our own good we need to know when to say no, and we need to know why it's often good to say so. Let me suggest some reasons why I think chastity, a proabstinence stance, makes sense as well as follows the biblical principle.

First, saying no is good for one's body. Chastity, restricting sexual activity to marriage, keeps us physically healthy. There's no better way to prevent unwanted pregnancy and sexually transmitted diseases.

Adults listening in on high school students' conversations often express astonishment at their casual accounts of their sexually active exploits as they talk about who was doing it with whom. When asked if they ever worry about AIDS or other health risks, they often just laugh. Many are too immature to realize that neither AIDS nor various sexually transmitted diseases are laughing matters.

Every year in America 1 in 10 teenage girls gets pregnant. Every year 2.5 million teens and perhaps 12 million Americans—33,000 a day!—contract a sexually transmitted disease. At the current rate 1 in 4 Americans now aged 15-55 will get some kind of sexually transmitted disease. And what do we tell our kids to do? What did the former surgeon general of the United States, Jocelyn Elders, urge? Practice "safe sex"! You can, generally speaking, prevent pregnancy with the pill, but it does nothing to protect one from sexually transmitted diseases. Condoms work—80 percent of the time.

In a college chapel service during a "Sexual Awareness" presentation, some pranksters had inflated a number of condoms with helium, so the devices were up against the ceiling when the speaker began his address. During the hour many of them floated down, eliciting a succession of laughs. The speaker handled it well, but neither he nor the students seemed to grasp the real truth revealed: condoms leak! They don't hold helium.

Nor do they protect wearers from tiny viruses and bacteria. Condoms grant no guarantees against AIDS or sexually transmitted diseases. They may be better than nothing, but they still resemble a game of Russian roulette. You have to be crazy to take a pistol with a bullet in it and pull the trigger. And you have to be crazy to trust condoms or other birth control devices to protect you from sexually transmitted diseases.

Second, say no for the good of your soul. Abstinence keeps us emotionally healthy. It protects us from feelings of guilt, of being used and abandoned, feelings that too often follow fornication. However well we fake it, we hurt when we're sexually manipulated. One thing that makes us uniquely human is our guilt feelings. Dogs and cats live perfectly carefree sex lives, "doing it" whenever and with whomever they feel like. But they apparently have no sense of even passing attachment to their partner in pleasure. We're not dogs and cats, however, even though it seems we easily ape their behavior.

Mark Twain once quipped, "Man is the only animal that blushes. Or needs to."[16] Now I admit that at times I wonder about this as does Rabbi Manis Friedman, who has titled his book *Doesn't Anyone Blush Anymore?* We may not blush, but we certainly feel loads of guilt.

Guys feel it. At a high school assembly, a well-known speaker was asked, "What do you most regret about your high school days?" Without hesitating, he said, "That I single-handedly destroyed a girl." That's guilt. That's the emotional cost of casual sex.

Women also pay an emotional price. A high school junior says, "I get upset when I see my friends losing their virginity to some guy they've just met. Later, after the guy's dumped them, they come to me and say, 'I wish I hadn't done it.'"

A ninth grade girl who slept with eight boys in junior high says, "I'm young, but I feel old."

Such are the sorrows of casual sex. Such are the reasons some of us never tire of warning young people not to cast away their health and holiness to enjoy momentary thrills.

However successfully we disguise it, we're haunted by our sexual sins. In his *Autobiography*, one of the greatest film directors, Ingmar Bergman, who married some of the most beautiful women in the world (as well as having affairs with many more), confessed: "Obsessed with a sexuality that forced me into constant infidelity, I was tormented by desire, fear, and a guilty conscience."[17] His lament sums up the ills of a soul tarnished by fornication—tormented by desire, fear, and guilt.

Be Holy, Wholly Spirit-filled

Along with the "Just say no" emphasis of this passage, however, there's a positive theme, the important message of God's will for our good, which is basic to Christian life. If we abstain from fornication, we find the good life, the holy life, the sanctified life for which we're designed.

It's good, for one thing, to learn self-control. Self-control, self-discipline, is basically what separates the men from the boys, the women from the girls. I really admire men like Art Monk, one of the best wide receivers ever to play professional football. For years he played for the Washington Redskins, and as an older man he managed to keep up with his younger teammates. He pursued perfection as a football player, joining his teammates for lunch but munching an apple while they inhaled cheeseburgers and fries. He lived a disciplined life, and he gained the rewards as a football star.

That's truth for life. We must submit to discipline in order to learn self-discipline in order to live as we really want to live. Folks who drift through life, doing what comes naturally whenever possible with whoever's around, never grow up. They're perpetual adolescents, controlled by their glands, never really free to be mature persons. But when we learn to control our body, we gain maturity, realizing what it means to be fully human, fully alive—wholly human, holy with life.

Still more, it's good to have moral borders, to respect legitimate sexual boundaries. That's because what we most deeply desire is not sexual pleasure but sexual intimacy, the kind of intimacy that's more than momentary sex, the kind of intimacy that thoroughly binds together two persons.[18]

Deep within us we long for personal intimacy. What we want in sex is an intimacy that lasts—and lasts. But what we lack all too often is the courage to reveal our inner self so as to establish real intimacy. We live, however, in an era of much promiscuous sexuality.

Indeed, some seek to eliminate the stigma of promiscuity, redefining it to indicate having sex with more than one person on a given day! So long as you limit yourself, on a daily basis, to one person (I guess that's monogamous-for-a-day, or 24-hour, monogamy), supposedly you're a righteous soul.

Yet underlying much of today's promiscuity there's this dual truth: we really crave intimacy, but we fear the truthfulness, the personal authenticity and transparency needed to sustain it. So we engage in passing, casual, non-threatening sexual adventures and affairs.

A woman wrote to "Dear Abby," complaining that she had been on the pill for two years while living with her boyfriend and thought he should pay half of the prescription bill—but she didn't feel she knew him well enough to discuss money. As one teenage woman confessed: "It is far easier to 'bare your bottom' than to 'bare your soul.'"[19]

But we must bare our souls to establish intimate personal relationships. There must be heart-to-heart truth at the heart of lasting, intimate unions. And that's exactly what the Bible teaches: fidelity makes us happy. The Bible's "restrictions concerning sexuality," says Rabbi Manis Friedman, "are not negative; they allow human passion, human sexuality to be a place of holiness. By saying 'no' to the wrong situation we create the 'yes' to the right emotion. That's the definition of marriage: permissible, holy passion to which we say 'yes,' and it does not violate our dwelling place."[20]

God would like for us to know the joy of holy living. That's why Jesus insisted we not lust for illicit sexual liaisons. Preeminently, we're taught to avoid lust because we're to live in the truth, and there's no truth in lust, for lust lies.

10

The Sanctity of Property

Years ago my wife and I built a log home on eight acres in a beautiful valley in eastern Kansas. It was secluded—and, consequently, vulnerable as well. One day during the first week of the school term, when both of us were away teaching, a burglar broke in and ransacked the place, looking for our hidden treasures. He dumped out all the drawers to see if we had stashed some cash. (Of ultimate insult to my wife, he dumped out her jewelry drawers—and took nothing!) He stole a 35 mm camera and lenses my father had given me, but that was all he found worth taking.

Now the financial value of what he took—especially since insurance covered much of the loss—was not terribly significant. The hours I had to spend repairing the door he crowbarred open were not all that precious. But the personal assault, the sense of being violated, endured. He stole more than a camera—he injured us! He made our world less safe, less homelike, less what it ought to be.

So I endorse the eighth commandment: "You shall not steal" (Exod. 20:15). The Hebrew word used, *ganab*, simply means "to take that which belongs to another without his or her consent or knowledge." Simple enough. None of us want people to steal our stuff. But, manifestly, they do. And folks do it in a variety of ways, ranging from force to fraud.

By Force

Thieves—bank robbers, muggers, burglars—simply take what they want by force. I heard about one bank robber who parked his car near the bank and left the engine running so as to expedite his getaway. An elderly lady noted the idling car, removed the keys, and locked it; then she followed the young man into the bank. While he was at the teller's window demanding cash, the lady tapped him on the shoulder and said: "Sonny, you should never leave your keys in the car—someone might steal it." Sufficiently flustered, he grabbed the keys and fled the bank.

Another bank robber hit the same bank three times. The FBI (Federal Bureau of Investigation) agent, talking to the teller after the last incident, said, "Did you notice anything special about the robber?"

"Yes," said the teller. "He seemed to be better dressed each time."

Such incidents, though perhaps humorous, remind us how routinely people steal by force, openly taking what's rightfully someone else's property. Clearly the Bible, as well as the civil law and common conscience, condemns this.

By Petty Theft

Few of us, I suppose, will engage in bank robbery or armed burglary. Most of us fear the police and prison sufficiently to refuse even to contemplate such acts. But ordinary persons are tempted to take what doesn't belong to them while shopping or on the job. Shoplifting statistics reveal that each year there are some 175 million incidents—equal to more than half the people in the nation. This is not to say over half the folks are shoplifting, of course, for some offenders commit scores of offenses—far more than their fair share. Amazingly, most shoplifters are middle-class people who don't need what they steal. They are driven to get something for nothing, seemingly inspired by the old hymn to "steal away, steal away"!

Then there are those who steal from their employers. Some stores write off as much as 50 percent of their profits to "inventory shrinkage." Employees, some analysts think, take three times as much merchandise as shoplifters. Insurance statistics suggest that perhaps as many as 30 percent of each year's failed businesses go under as a result of employees stealing, ironically destroying the very source of their livelihood.

To deal with this situation, an innovative outfit in New York, calling itself THEFT (an acronym for The Honest Employees Fooling Thieves), places one of its specialists, a young actor, on a site, where he or she works for a while as a typical employee. Then he gets caught stealing—and with lots of screaming and threats, the boss fires him. Normal employees, unaware of the plant, get the message. For a while at least, thefts decline. "Hire Someone to Fire" is the firm's motto.

By Fraud

If possible, those who steal by fraud are even worse than those who steal by force. Embezzlers, swindlers, con men who exploit the weak are usually the big-time thieves who do the most harm. As Joy Davidman said, "The confidence men are the aristocrats of American crime."[1] They're the ones who manipulate things by "rigging contracts, bribing officials, finding loopholes in the tax laws, playing tricks with foreign exchange, lying about the goods we sell and selling trash!"[2] They're also the politicians who manipulate laws and monetary policies to insure their next election, raking in moneys thereby.

It's an old, old story. Most of you have heard that in 1624 a Dutchman, Peter Minuit, bought Manhattan Island from the Indians for $24—which was quite a steal of a deal.

But actually the Indians who sold Manhattan didn't own it. The sellers were the Canarsees, native to Brooklyn rather than Manhattan. They simply conned Minuit and departed with the loot. The real residents of Manhattan, the Weckquaesgeeks, were just shoved aside. But the Canarsees were real businessmen. They not only sold Manhattan but also sold Staten Island, which wasn't theirs either. And they sold it six times to various groups! (Those Canarsees didn't need a master's degree in business administration or a seat in Congress to know how to turn a quick buck.)

Let's go back even farther. Remember how King Ahab wanted a vineyard near his palace in Jezreel, but the owner, Naboth, refused to sell it, saying, "The LORD forbid that I should give you the inheritance of my fathers" (1 Kings 21:3)? Frustrated, "Ahab went home, sullen and angry," and "lay on his bed sulking and refused to eat. [But then] his wife Jezebel came in and asked him, 'Why are you so sullen? Why won't you eat?'" (vv. 4-5). In response, Ahab told his sad story. Then "Jezebel his wife said, 'Is this how you act as king over Israel? Get up and eat! Cheer up. I'll get you the vineyard of Naboth the Jezreelite'" (v. 7).

So she initiated a plan whereby Naboth was falsely accused and was stoned to death, and Ahab got his vineyard. So the world turns! Kings and queens do things that way. Powerful people, rich people, Wall Street gurus, and con men scheme and manipulate and defraud. White-collar crime pervades the business world. Bank robbers usually get a few thousand dollars at best. Inside traders on Wall Street get millions and millions. One man said, "The marketplace is a jungle. The big cats stalk their prey, the jackals lie in wait for the weak, and the rats fight over the leavings." With a strange perversity "The Golden Rule of the world of economics has been distorted to 'Do your neighbor before he does you.'"

Plagiary

We also steal when we claim other people's poems, songs, and essays and use them as our own. Were we to steal an artist's statue, it would be obvious we had taken something that belongs to him. But when we take a composer's lyrics, or a scholar's research, or a journalist's story, or a preacher's sermon, we're stealing just as much.

One of the most prominent preachers 50 years ago was Harry Emerson Fosdick. One Sunday while on vacation, he went to a small church in Maine and found himself listening to one of his own sermons, delivered by a young pastor who pretended it was his own. Following the message, Fosdick praised the sermon and asked the young man how long it had taken him to prepare it. "About 3 hours," said the young man.

"You're a fast worker," Fosdick replied. "It took me 21 hours."

Amazingly enough, in view of this incident, one of Fosdick's biographers found that the master preacher, who took offense at the young man's plagiary, often used quotations himself without acknowledging their source.[3] More recently, Theodore Pappas says, "We now know that Martin Luther King, Jr., routinely plagiarized not only his college, seminary, and graduate school essays, including his doctoral dissertation, but many of his most famous speeches and published works as well, including the legendary 'I Have a Dream' oration."[4]

Add to King such names as Sen. Joe Biden, Alex Haley, Dee Brown, Gail Sheehy, and Maya Angelou, and you begin to fathom the depths of the problem.

It's now an industry, this business of plagiary! In every issue of *Rolling Stone*, a magazine widely read by college-age young people, one finds ads that promise first-rate term papers for a fee. "Term Paper Assistance. 1,600 Papers Available! 306-page catalog—rush $2.00," says one.

Here's another: "Term Paper Blues? Term Paper Assistance. Catalog of 19,278 research papers. Research Assistance also provides custom research and thesis assistance. Our staff of 75 professional writers, each writing in his field of expertise, can assist you with all your research needs."[5] The magazine's own hypocritical posturing stands revealed in its ads, for *Rolling Stone* regularly berates dishonest politicians and defrocked preachers while urging its readers to cheat in school!

Years ago one of my students apparently bought one of these papers. He was one of those guys who came to class about half the time, and what work he did was hardly adequate. But his term paper discussed heavyweight philosophers such as Hegel. And the footnotes were most impressive—even citing lengthy quotations in German! To test his honesty, on the final exam I prepared some individualized questions for this student, asking him to explain some of the terms used so smoothly in the paper and to translate some of the German. He knew nothing about his own citations. And he failed the class. Sometimes we teachers are brighter than we look.

Teachers know cheating occurs. Around a third of high school and college students admit to cheating. It's almost an epidemic in American schools. When students cheat, of course, they steal from their fellow students who do honest work. For cheating in school, plagiarizing research papers, violates the eighth commandment. When we steal a person's words, when we take and use another's ideas, we steal what's in fact most truly his or hers. Even worse, when we steal, we torpedo our own integrity. The damage we do when we cheat most seriously damages our own souls.

So the words of Madison Sarratt, dean of Vanderbilt University, who taught freshman math for years, should challenge us: "Today I am going to give you two examinations—one in trigonometry and one in honesty. I hope you will pass both of them. But if you must fail one, let it be trigonometry. There are many good men in the world who cannot pass an examination in trigonometry, but there are no good men who cannot pass an examination in honesty."[6] The world needs a few good men and women—honest men and women. So *don't steal!*

NEW TESTAMENT INTERNALIZATION: LIVING HONESTLY BY MAKING AN HONEST LIVING

While running for his party's presidential nomination in 1960, John F. Kennedy visited a coal mine in West Virginia, where he talked with one of the miners. "Is it true you're the son of one of the wealthiest men?" the miner asked.

Kennedy admitted he was multimillionaire Joseph Kennedy's son.

"Is it true," the miner continued, "that you've never wanted for anything and had everything you wanted?"

"I guess so," said Kennedy.

"Is it true you've never done a day's work with your hands all your life?" Kennedy nodded yes.

"Well, let me tell you this," said the miner. "You haven't missed a thing."[7]

So it seems to lots of us who earn a living by daily toil. Working often seems a drag, a bore, a necessary evil perhaps, but still nothing to relish. We're a bit like a guy who was asked, "How long you been working here?" who responded, "Ever since the boss threatened to fire me."

Whether we like it or not, work is important. In fact, it's part of living honestly—making an honest living. In business writer Peter Drucker's opinion, that's precisely what's missing in the workplace.

When you look for New Testament amplifications on the Old Testament commandment against stealing, you find, amazingly enough, admonitions to *work*. Paul said, "He who has been stealing must steal no longer, but must work, doing something useful with his own hands, that he may have something to share with those in need" (Eph. 4:28).

Make Goods That Are Good

Oscar Wilde once said, "Work is the refuge of people who have nothing better to do."[8] Now that's a clever comment, but it's untrue. A bit more realistically, Ogden Nash quipped, "If you don't want to work, you have to work in order to earn enough money so that you won't have to work."[9]

In truth, we've nothing better to do than *good* work. We work because we need to help meet the world's need for good stuff, the goods we need in order to live well. We should work so as to add goods—good things—to our world. As men and women created in God's image, we are creative. We can make good stuff that makes our world a better place, more abundant and beautiful.

Unfortunately, one of the negative dividends of the industrial revolution is this: it took from most of us the opportunity to develop our skills as craftsmen. When we work in an office punching a computer keyboard, or in a factory screwing taps on bolts, we rarely feel creative. We feel as if we're reduced to robots; we become part of a vast machine that is spitting out identical items for mass markets.

Yet we feel, deep in our hearts, that we should do creative work, artistic work. "Originality and the feeling of one's own dignity are achieved only through work and struggle,"[10] said Fyodor Dostoyevsky. Ananda Coomaraswamy asserted, "The artist is not a special kind of man, but every man is a special kind of artist."[11] That's so true. Admittedly few of us are Michelangelo-type artists. Most of us have the limited kind of artistic skills that should develop in the work we do.

I'm not a great writer, such as Ernest Hemingway, but as a teacher I need to write as well as I can. I'm no Billy Graham as a preacher, but when preaching I must speak as well as I can. Doing so unleashes whatever artistic talent is latent within me. The world and the world's peoples need the goods that can be made only by workers who work well, doing so with a dedication to live honestly by making an honest living.

Do Good!

Let's turn to another biblical passage. In 2 Thessalonians Paul directed his readers:

> In the name of the Lord Jesus Christ, we command you, brothers, to keep away from every brother who is idle and does not live according to the teaching you received from us. For you yourselves know how you ought to follow our example. We were not idle when we were with you, nor did we eat anyone's food without paying for it. On the contrary, we worked night and day, laboring and toiling so that we would not be a burden to any of you. We did this, not because we do not have the right to such help, but in order to make ourselves a model for you to follow. For even when we were with you, we gave you this rule: "If a man will not work, he shall not eat" (3:6-10).

One of the great Christian movements of all time was launched by Benedict in the sixth century. His followers, the Benedictine monks, did much of the missionary-evangelistic work that converted the barbarians, making Europe a Christian place 500 years later. The motto of the Benedictines is this: *oro et labore*—pray and work. To work is to pray. Work well and pray well. Pray well and work well. To be a blessing, to truly bless our world, we must work and pray, pray and work, to the glory of God the Father.

Not only is work good for our own sense of self-worth, but also work is important because it helps us overcome our own self-centeredness, our continual tendency to live only for ourselves. By its very nature, work is a communal endeavor. We build bonds with others by joining together to make things.

Athletes, we all know, work together for the good of the team, submerging their identities in that of the group. Almost immediately after being appointed the new coach of the New England Patriots, Bill Parsells made this clear in his first public speech: only *team players* need show up for training camp. He wanted more than a star-studded team; he wanted a championship team. And you never win championships with a bunch of prima donna athletes strutting their stuff on the field.

I read about a woman who took her son with her to work one day. She had talked with him about the office before, and when she mentioned the possibility of his spending a day with her, he seemed genuinely excited. Though ordinarily shy, he seemed eager to meet each of her coworkers when she introduced them. After a day on the job, however, he was clearly unhappy. Going home, the mother asked her son what was troubling him. Finally he opened up and expressed his disappointment. "I never got to see the clowns you said you worked with," he complained.[12]

Too often that's our attitude. We see work as a necessary evil, something we do merely to make money, and we see our coworkers as folks to be tolerated—folks clearly less competent than we are. Our incurable self-centeredness soils our attitudes and behaviors in our workplace.

That's the thrust of Paul's admonition to the Thessalonians: Do your duty! Work to sustain the social bonds we all need. Doing one's share, contributing to the good of the whole, is one way to give yourself away. So not only must we work ourselves, but also we must insist that others work, and we must where possible devise ways for them to find work.

I confess that I'm by nature an introvert, a person who craves solitude, easily content doing things on my own. I don't particularly need or desire to work together with other people. I'm temperamentally a long-distance runner rather than a basketball player. If you have something you need done, just give me an individual assignment and let me do it. And I think folks like me have a certain role to play, a clear niche to fill, in the grand scheme of things.

But it's for this reason that it's good for me to work at a college. Here I must interact with and support faculty colleagues. I must follow the policies established by the administration. I must teach the classes others have decided students need, not simply those I happen to enjoy. I must study and grade papers and help students learn what they need to learn, not necessarily what appeals to me. I'm not really free to do my own thing as a teacher.

And that's good for my soul, as well as good for my world, for I need to work for others—and my work as a teacher requires me to do precisely that. I contribute, in however small a way, to the good of those around me by working *with* others for a cause that's bigger than any one of us.

Be Good

We are, of course, regularly reminded of those who are unemployed. President Calvin Coolidge once said, "When more and more people are thrown out of work, unemployment results."[13] Well, yes—how profound! And how awful! Folks need to work to feel they are worthy persons. The Spanish philosopher José Ortega y Gasset wrote:

> An *unemployed* existence is a worse negation of life than death itself. Because to live means to have something definite to do—a mission to fulfill—and in the measure in which we avoid setting our life to something, we make it empty. . . . Human life, by its very nature, has to be dedicated to something.[14]

More succinctly, Albert Camus declared, "Without work all life goes rotten."[15] So we really don't do anyone a favor by putting him or her on welfare. The Bible clearly urges us to give alms, to share with the needy. But Paul also makes it clear that we should give to people to help them through a crisis, not to free them from working themselves.

In *Why America Doesn't Work,* Chuck Colson and Jack Eckerd describe conditions in Holland. The nation has one of the world's most generous welfare states—so generous, in fact, that one in six workers stays home, claiming "benefits for psychological or physical disabilities"! Now don't dash for the next plane to Holland! Just across the border, in Germany, only half as many claim similar disabilities. And if you want to, study the economic differences between Holland and Germany. As one Dutch industrialist lamented, "Our welfare state was meant to provide a safety net, but it has turned into a hammock."[16]

So too in America. We hear lots about the energy crisis, but perhaps the biggest "energy crisis" in this country occurs each Monday morning. Few of the TGIF (Thank Goodness It's Friday) folks jump out of bed anxious to make their contribution to the world's welfare. Yet that's what we're called to do.

That's simply the biblical way. Unlike the ancient Greeks, who rather despised manual labor, the Hebrews always stressed its dignity. "He who does not teach his son a trade," said the rabbis, "teaches him to steal." So Paul, a "Hebrew of the Hebrews" (Phil. 3:5, kjv), draws upon his own heritage, the Jewish tradition, urging believers (many of them slaves) to work industriously.

That Jewish attitude characterized the new nation of Israel that emerged in Palestine following World War II. David Ben-Gurion, one of the new nation's greatest leaders, said, "We don't consider manual work as a curse, or a bitter necessity, not even as a means of making a living. We consider it as a high human function, as a basis of human life, the most dignified thing in the life of a human being, and which ought to be free, creative."[17]

Good work gives us dignity. Good work helps us become what we're designed to be. Good work enables us to realize our potential as human beings. Work, in fact, contributes to our sanctification. So, as noted artist Eric Gill says, "The object of human life is man's sanctification, labour being the means of life in the appointed means to holiness and thus to beatitude."[18]

Concert violinists know the difference between a violin and a Stradivarius violin. Centuries ago, Antonio Stradivari simply made the best violins ever made. As translated by George Eliot, Stradivari explained his commitment to his task, to his work:

> When any master holds 'twixt chin and hand a violin of mine, he will be glad that Stradivari lived, made violins, and made them of the best. . . . For while God gives them skill I give them instruments to play upon, God choosing me to help him. . . . If my hand slacked I should rob God—since he is fullest good—leaving blank instead of violins. . . . he could not make Antonio Stradivari's violins without Antonio.[19]

God, give us more Antonios whose work blesses our world!

11

The Sanctity of Our Word

OLD TESTAMENT FOUNDATION: NO FALSE WITNESSES

We live in a litigious society. "Litigious," if you don't recognize the word, means continually taking others to court, launching lawsuits like arrows to rectify injustices or reclaim elusive "rights."

Chuck Colson's *Prison Fellowship Newsletter* not long ago told of a burglar in California who fell through a skylight while robbing a school. Alleging himself permanently disabled, he sued the school for negligence. (I guess skylights should be designed to hold 200 pounds!) A compassionate court apparently felt his pain and awarded him a total of $260,000 in damages, plus a $1,200 monthly stipend. Now that's the kind of crime that pays!

Then there's a woman who claimed to have mysterious psychic powers. She developed some physical ailment, sought treatment, and the hospital administered a CAT (*c*omputerized *a*xial *t*omography) scan, which involved injecting dye into the brain. As a result—she claims—she lost her psychic powers. Then she successfully sued the hospital and won $1 million in damages.[1] If you think about that a bit, you might question her psychic powers, for surely she could have foreseen the CAT scan risks and refused to allow it.

One of Britain's greatest lawyers, F. E. Smith, once cross-examined a man who claimed his arm had been permanently disabled by a bus driver's negligence. Smith first said, "Will you please show us how high you can lift your arm now?" The man struggled, obviously in great pain, unable to raise his arm to shoulder level. "Thank you," said Smith. "Now, would you please show us how high you could raise it before the accident?" Eager to impress the court, the young man fully extended his arm aloft—and, of course, lost his suit in the process.[2]

In all too many such cases there's more at stake than money. What's at stake is truth—truthfulness in court. For when folks lie in court, when they commit perjury in a court of law, not only do they defraud somebody, but also they subvert one of the best guarantors of a good society: a fair judicial system. All good societies need an honest and equitable legal system.

So with that in mind, let's consider the ninth commandment: "You shall not give false testimony against your neighbor" (Exod. 20:16), or, in a more ancient translation, "Thou shalt not bear false witness against thy neighbour" (KJV). If we're to walk with God, if we're to remain in covenant relationship with Him—which is, we must always remember, the purpose of the Ten Commandments, the "10 steps to freedom"—we must never bear false witness against our neighbor, especially in formal, public, legal ways. What this commandment forbids is clear: deliberate, false, malicious testimony. That's made clear a bit later in Exodus, which says, "Do not spread false reports. Do not help a wicked man by being a malicious witness. Do not follow the crowd in doing wrong. When you give testimony in a lawsuit, do not pervert justice by siding with the crowd, and do not show favoritism to a poor man in his lawsuit" (23:1-3).

We who observe celebrated criminal trials, such as

that of O. J. Simpson, easily understand the importance of truthful witnesses. A wicked man may escape punishment if witnesses lie for him. A good man may be punished if witnesses lie against him. Juries who cave in to public opinion, judges who favor the economically disadvantaged, all cooperate in falsifying the truth, dislodging the balance of justice.

Intent Constitutes a Lie

In the 1960s, when young folks marched in the streets and dreamed of making the world a better place, one of the oft repeated slogans was "You can't trust anyone over 30." As the marchers aged, of course, that creed quickly lost its luster!

Another slogan in that era said: "Tell it like it is." That's still a good goal. It's always been so, for it's a reasonably clear definition of truth. I like that motto. It's admirable and worth embracing. I always want to tell it like it is; I want to tell the truth. But if telling the truth means describing things as they are, precisely detailing details, most of us fail daily. Many of us struggle to tell it like it is exactly. We're less than candid at times, we often err, we disguise the truth to shield others' feelings, and we do in fact fail to state the facts.

Without intending to, I sometimes speak untruths when I speak as college chaplain in chapel! In one message, differentiating the genetic characteristics of the sexes, I averred that the genetic process that produces a male of our species involves an XY mating with a YY. In fact, I should have said an XX mates with a YY—as one of our biology professors reminded me immediately after chapel. Now I realize that I should be more careful, especially when I'm checking my facts in a reference work; but when I'm speaking, my mind too frequently slips some cogs.

In the process of teaching I sometimes mislead my students with false information and later feel utterly humiliated by my errors. Since I generally have a good memory, and since I think teaching is more than reading prepared scripts for lectures, I seem predestined to commit such errors. And truthfully, I fail to tell the full truth in such instances. I feel guilty for such failures, and I duly admit them when necessary. But I don't really *intend* to err. My obligation to tell the truth is obvious. My ability always to tell it like it is slips and slides as I try my best to do so. Fortunately, for me at least, the ninth commandment has little to do with my inadvertent failures to tell it like it is.

This commandment is not necessarily concerned with whether you say "fine" or "OK" when I ask, "How ya doin'?" It's not terribly concerned about the scientific accuracy of our efforts to make others feel good when we praise them. It's not concerned with the fact we deceive one another in games and practical jokes. Nor does it insist we abandon rhetorical hyperboles (as Jesus used in many of His parables) designed to elicit a laugh or make a point. In other words, there's lots of latitude in our discourse, and we needn't worry overmuch about always telling it like it is. What we must ever avoid is deliberately telling untruths that harm our neighbors.

No Perjury, No False and Malicious Untruths Allowed

What this commandment forbids is deliberately giving false witness, when the clearly intended testimony is in fact untrue. A contemporary rabbi, Robert Kahn, says, "The Bible is pitiless toward the perjurer. When you stop to think about it, there is probably no more calculatedly vicious crime."[3] In public, legal, courtroom testimony, truth must always be told. Still more: even outside the courtroom the Bible forbids slander—the malicious defamation of another.

In an article in the *San Diego Union*, Tom Blair described a scene in a superior court.

Two men were on trial for armed robbery. An eye-witness took the stand, and the prosecutor moved carefully. "So, you say you were on the scene when the robbery took place?"

"Yes," the man said.

"And you saw a vehicle leave at a high rate of speed?"

"Yes."

"And did you observe the occupants?"

"Yes, two men."

"And," the prosecutor boomed, "are those two men present in court today?" At this point, the two defendants sealed their fate. They raised their hands.

Truth to tell, they should have! For in court, folks should tell the truth, even when it hurts. If you lie in court, it's called perjury—and perjury is a felony. Folks serve hard time in prison for telling lies in court.

Similarly, in our daily lives, telling lies in public—while perhaps not perjury in the narrow sense—betrays one's trust. When President Ronald Reagan nominated Robert Bork for a position on the United States Supreme Court, a devious coalition of special interest groups fabricated lies designed to deny him Senate approval. Assuming Bork told the truth (and I believe he did) in his fine book *The Tempting of America,* members of the Senate Judiciary Committee (notably Sen. Ted Kennedy), abortion rights organizations, and the liberal media deliberately spread fabrications and false rumors and accusations concerning him. In the time given and the limited resources he had, Bork couldn't turn back the avalanche of accusations. So he was denied a seat on the nation's highest court.

Tragically, in the political arena, where we as citizens most need our leaders to speak the truth, lies are routinely told. Dictators deny the truth. Adolf Hitler declared, "In the size of the lie is always contained a certain factor of credulity, since the great masses of the people . . . will more easily fall victims to the great lie than to a small one."[4]

Such strategies are not limited to dictatorial regimes. In "democratic republics" leaders too often mislead the people in order to remain their leaders. Knowing he would involve the nation in war as soon as possible, President Franklin D. Roosevelt, determined to get reelected in 1940, promised: "I have said this before, but I shall say it again and again: Your boys are not going to be sent into any foreign wars."[5] He was, of course, elected—and American boys soon shed their blood on battlefields around the world.

In 1964 President Lyndon Johnson, knowing the American people wanted to stay out of war in Vietnam, portrayed presidential candidate Barry Goldwater as a warmonger poised to fling atom bombs at any shadowy foe and said, "The first responsibility, the only issue in this campaign, the only thing you ought to be concerned about at all is: Who can best keep the peace."[6] Once elected, he led us into the quagmire of Vietnam, one of the worst wars in this nation's history.

In the midst of a great outcry over the nation's financial deficit in the early 1990s, *Washington Post* columnist David Broder pointed out the real "deficit" United States President Bill Clinton should address: *trust.* To make his point, he noted that a Republican ad claimed candidate Clinton could fulfill his promises only by "raising taxes on every family making more than $36,000 a year." Indignant, Clinton called the ad "blatantly false," a "disgrace," a "shameless" move to get votes. Once elected, however, Broder notes, Clinton glibly proposed taxing families making over $30,000, claiming "unexpected" budgetary matters forced him to do so.[7]

In her 1994 campaign for the United States Senate, Dianne Feinstein proudly pointed to her support of the balanced budget amendment. Her printed and television campaign ads made it a major part of her appeal. No sooner was she returned to the Senate, however, than she broke her word and voted against the amendment, which failed by one vote in the Senate in 1995. False witnesses!

In their public role, one wherein they swear to uphold the Constitution and rightly lead this nation, our leaders simply should not bear false witness. They should not lie to the American people. That they routinely do so is a sad commentary on the moral morass of the nation. Just contrast some of our recent leaders with our first United States president, George Washington, who said, rather accurately in the judgment of most historians, "I do not recollect . . . that in the course of my life I ever forfeited my word, or broke a promise to anyone."[8] Now that's a man worth making president!

Finally, breaking the ninth commandment entails malice—a lie must be malicious, as well as intentional and clearly untrue.

Malicious untruths attack persons. As Sissela Bok insists in *Lying: Moral Choice in Public and Private Life*, "Deceit and violence—these are the two forms of deliberate assault on human beings."[9]

Italian dictator Benito Mussolini said, "Our motto must be to lie in order to conquer."[10] And so he sought to construct his fascist regime, rooted in and riddled with lies.

Like many moderns, Mussolini seemed to inhale some of the ideas of a German philosopher, atheist Friedrich Nietzsche, who declared: "A great man—what is he? . . . He rather lies than tells the truth; it requires more spirit and *will*. There is a solitude within him that is inaccessible to praise or blame, his own justice that is beyond appeal."[11]

Yet when we shatter the trust we need in order to live with one another, and we follow Nietzsche's admonition and impose our willed untruths on our world, we destroy it. For lies poison our world. And we're as guilty for poisoning the moral atmosphere as we are for poisoning the air.

Several years ago I had a student who tried to live according to Nietzsche's teaching. In a class where I require reports describing the past week's reading, I noticed a section of his third report that duplicated his second report. Then his fourth report duplicated almost all his third week's report! When I confronted him with this, he wrote a long letter explaining how he could, with effort, *imagine* how someone like me might imagine he was cheating. But he declared he wasn't, however identical the two reports appeared. His *saying* so made it so, in his mirror-encased private world.

Later he turned in a report claiming to discuss Nietzsche's *Birth of Tragedy.* I suspected that nothing in the report dealt with Nietzsche's book, since the student was waxing eloquent about the kinds of things you find on book jacket covers. But I took the time to read the entire book and confirmed my suspicions. We had an interesting confrontation. At first he claimed he had read the book, but it soon became evident (since he could answer none of my questions) that he knew nothing about it.

Then he shifted his approach, arguing that it didn't matter what he read or even if he had read what he claimed. What mattered was what he thought—and his thoughts, of course, were marvelous. Then he made an astounding claim: looking at the side of a building, he said, "If I see dancing girls on the wall, they're there, whether you see them or not."

Had I thought quickly, I would have pulled out my grade book and said, "Here's your name—you see A, and I see F."

My student, you see, deliberately tried to deceive me. He wanted to get a good grade without working. In doing so, he was willing to harm indirectly the students who were doing honest work. In lying, he corrupted the whole academic climate, just as witnesses who lie corrupt the whole judicial climate. And neither can please the Lord!

NEW TESTAMENT INTERNALIZATION: TRUTHFUL TONGUES

A first grade teacher in Belvedere, California, Judith Frost Stark, elicits creative responses from her students by asking them to complete familiar proverbs in their own words. Some of the kids' responses are printed in her book, *Don't Cross Your Bridges Before . . . You Pay the Toll*. The surprising twists kids put on familiar proverbs illustrate the power of words cleverly spoken.

Tongue's Power—Nothing's Stronger, in Fact

Words make our world. Think about it: *Words make our world!* There's nothing more worthwhile than a word. Nothing's more world-shaping or world-shaking than a word. Nothing's stronger than the tongue. Most parts of the human body slowly atrophy in time. Arthritis and tendinitis assail us older folks, limiting the action of our knees and shoulders. But the tongue stays forever young. The tongue's too strong to wear out ever.

So when we turn from the Old Testament, where the ninth commandment insists we not bear false witness against our neighbor, to the New Testament, where the Law is internalized through the presence of the Lord Jesus through the power of His Holy Spirit, we find a sustained concern that we speak rightly about our neighbor. As Christians, we're called not simply to speak the truth— we're called to "speak . . . the truth in love" (Eph. 4:15).

Jesus' brother James in his powerful little letter declared, "If anyone considers himself religious and yet does not keep a tight rein on his tongue, he deceives himself and his religion is worthless" (1:26). In the third chapter he picks up the same theme: "Not many of you should presume to be teachers, my brothers, because you know that we who teach will be judged more strictly. We all stumble in many ways. If anyone is never at fault in what he says, he is a perfect man, able to keep his whole body in check" (vv. 1-2).

There's Power to Kill in the Tongue

Continuing, James notes that we can control horses and ships, "but no man can tame the tongue. It is a restless evil, full of deadly poison" (v. 8).

When I was young, a child offended or hurt by another's words often chanted, "Sticks and stones may break my bones, but words will never hurt me." It's a statement you still hear on playgrounds. Like many popular sayings, this one expresses a partial truth: sticks and stones really do break bones. But it suggests something utterly untrue in saying words won't hurt, for while sticks and stones may break bones, they break *only* bones, while words may scar forever.

"Death and life," says Prov. 18:21, "are in the power of the tongue" (KJV). Our words are mightier than machine guns; bullets take lives, destroying bodies, but words penetrate deeper, destroying souls. To modify a childhood taunt, "Sticks and stones may break our bones—but words can shred my soul!"

There's Also Power to Heal with the Tongue

So powerful is it, in fact, that "with the tongue we praise our Lord and Father, and with it we curse men, who have been made in God's likeness. Out of the same mouth come praise and cursing. My brothers, this should not be" (James 3:9-10).

Though we're tempted to dwell on the negative powers of the tongue, we must note there's also power to heal, power in praise. Though the phrases of James largely warn us to avoid doing harm, the underlying intent of the passage is positive. Just as we bless God with our tongue, so we can bless our neighbor in the same way. What a wonderful opportunity each of us has every day literally to make someone's day with our tongue!

We often say, repeating Napoléon's quip, that "a picture's worth a thousand words," thus indicating words' poverty compared with visual images. Again this is partially true, for we certainly learn information better from pictures than words. Napoléon no doubt understood battle plans better by looking at a map than by listening to a corporal's report. When working on a car's engine, I certainly need illustrations, diagrams—even cartoons—that clarify mechanical matters for me.

Yet it's also true that a word may be worth a thousand pictures. No pictures inwardly warm my heart like the words "I love you" on the lips of my wife. No pictures evoke creative insights within my mind that come with the power of words rightly spoken in conversations with friends and students. No pictures touch my soul as do the lyrics of some Bob Dylan songs or T. S. Eliot poems or C. S. Lewis Narnian scenes.

We often say, "Actions speak louder than words," or "What you do speaks so loudly I can't hear a word you say." This is certainly true. Actions are *louder,* more arresting, more concrete—not necessarily better, not truer. When our actions belie our words, we stand guilty of lying, and our words lose their value.

Yet, truth to tell, words often speak more loudly than actions. Actions may be more visible, may affect us powerfully at the *moment,* but they do not enter into and inspire and inwardly mold our souls. What you do for me, be it ever so generous and kind, makes my environment more comfortable. But words spoken to me do more than improve my world. Words may be more life-giving and inspiring than actions. Just as oxygen enters my lungs and thence into my blood, so words enter into the pulsating circulatory system of my spirit. As I hear and respond to words, they make me who I am.

That truth is evident in the coaching career of Bill

Walsh, one of the most successful football coaches in American history. Walsh demanded much from his athletes, he acknowledges, but to get men really to perform, he had to motivate them. The best way to motivate football players, he found, was not with threats or bribes. He discovered that "the simplest way to motivate people is plain, old-fashioned praise, handed out in the right way at the right time."[12]

Though money certainly motivates us—and National Football League (NFL) players and coaches are well paid—money's not enough, Walsh says; "Money talks, but it doesn't always say enough."[13] Positive, powerful words do what money fails to do. Such praise must be precise, properly given, thoroughly truthful. When rightly uttered, words of praise prompt men to perform in accord with their highest potential. "You can be damned by faint praise, and you can sabotage yourself with effusive praise," he concludes. "Or you can master the art of high praise."[14]

It's obvious that words are some of the most important realities of our world. We make words, and words make us. It's critical that we use them wisely and well. Listen to what C. S. Lewis says in *Reflections on the Psalms:*

> The world rings with praise—lovers praising their mistresses, readers their favorite poet, walkers praising the countryside, players praising their favorite game. . . . I had not noticed how the humblest, and at the same time most balanced and capacious, minds, praised most, while the cranks, misfits and malcontents praised least.[15]

Let me repeat and italicize some of Lewis's words: *"The humblest, and at the same time most balanced and capacious, minds, praised most, while the cranks, misfits and malcontents praised least."* The best athletes are most likely to commend another athlete's performance. I've heard Magic Johnson talk about rival basketball players such as Michael Jordan or Larry Bird, and he always commended them.

I've heard Joe Montana (perhaps the greatest to ever play his position) discuss other NFL quarterbacks, and he easily praised them. He knows we know he's good, so he's at ease complimenting his rivals.

Still more, Lewis says: *"Praise almost seems to be inner health made audible"* (emphasis added).[16] If we have a good heart, if we really love people, we'll tend to praise rather than find fault with them. I think my wife would tell you that I rarely criticize her—*never* in public, if I'm aware of what I'm saying—and rarely in private. That's because I love her and rarely find fault with her. Since I love *her* so much, things she *does* don't particularly disturb me. When we criticize others more ruthlessly than we do our spouses, it probably means we love them less, not that they're full of more faults.

In one of their most valuable books, Gary Smalley and John Trent emphasize the importance of "the blessing."[17] The first element of blessing others is "meaningful touch." They tell a story about Dorothy, who took a speech class in a university. The first day they were all asked to introduce themselves, telling something they both liked and disliked about themselves. When it came Dorothy's turn, she sighed, pulled back her long red hair that covered part of her face, and revealed a large red birthmark. "That," she said, "should show you what I don't like about myself."

The professor, a devout Christian, responded by going to her desk, giving her a hug, kissing her on the birthmark, saying, "That's OK, Honey—God and I still think you're beautiful."

At that Dorothy began crying. And she cried for 20 minutes. Finally she got control and said to the professor: "I've wanted so much for someone to hug me and say what you said. Why couldn't my parents do that? My mother wouldn't even touch my face."[18]

We reach out and touch and in the process heal with

our love. We can bless our world with a touch—and with our words that touch the heart!

We really do need to hear words of blessing from folks who care for us. Abraham spoke to bless his son Isaac, and Isaac spoke a blessing for his son Jacob. The right words at the right time may well inspire a lifetime.

During my first year of graduate study at the University of Oklahoma, I enrolled in a class on western American history, taught by one of the nation's most respected Indian historians, Donald J. Berthrong. After the midterm examination, I was doing some research in a special collections section of the library. Dr. Berthrong walked by me, paused, and said, "That was a fine exam you wrote for me, Mr. Reed." That's all he said, but those words helped me believe I would make it through the demanding course of studies prescribed for Ph.D. candidates. Berthrong *blessed* me with his words. His words made a difference for me.

One of the great 17th-century dramatists, Ben Jonson, wrote, "Language most shows a man: / Speak, that I may see thee."[19] When you go to a doctor for a physical checkup, he often examines your tongue. The color of the tongue, the texture of the tongue reveals something about the health of the body. So, too, the words we speak reveal more than we suspect about the health of our soul.

When we praise others, not only do we reveal a healthy soul, but also we make our soul healthy. Praise can become a way of life if we determine to be a blessing by blessing those around us.

12

The Sanctity of Satisfaction

OLD TESTAMENT FOUNDATION: DO NOT COVET

When Israel's first king, Saul, backslid and fell from grace, the old prophet Samuel set out to find and anoint his successor. Intent on selecting one of them king, he checked out Jesse's sons, first noting Eliab, the firstborn, who seemed a good prospect. "But the LORD said to Samuel, 'Do not consider his appearance or his height, for I have rejected him. . . . Man looks at the outward appearance, but the LORD looks at the heart'" (1 Sam. 16:7).

God sees the heart! You and I easily evaluate others by their appearance—by the clothes they wear or the color of their hair—but God looks at the heart. We tend to think like Joseph Kennedy, father of a modern political dynasty, who told his kids, "It's not what you are, but what people think you are, that really counts."

And if you're a Joe Kennedy (or one of his opportunist kids), that's true, for the world generally judges by appearances. "Fake it till you make it" flies well in practice as well as in slogans in many circles. On the contrary, Gregory of Nazianzus, one of the fourth-century "Cappadocian" church fathers, insisted we embrace this principle: *esse quam videri*—we should *be* rather than merely *appear* to be.

What ultimately matters is that we really be what we ought to be.

Thus, the Ten Commandments, the 10 steps to freedom, the 10 Words whereby God sought to establish and sustain a covenant relationship with His people, begin and end with the heart, the inner self secluded from direct observation. As God's folks, we're offered the prospects of a heart set free. First of all, "You shall have no other gods before me"; second, "You shall not covet." The tenth commandment says, "You shall not covet your neighbor's house. You shall not covet your neighbor's wife, or his manservant or maidservant, his ox or donkey, or anything that belongs to your neighbor" (Exod. 20:17).

The Hebrew word translated "covet" means to "desire, yearn for, lust after" something or someone, seeking self-gratification. It's a strong word, meaning to launch a process designed to attain one's ends—a process that begins with assent to a plan. There's a Latin phrase that succinctly captures it: *libido dominandi.* It's the will to power, the desire to possess. Covetousness is an inner assent, an intent to get something we have no right to have. More than mere wishful thinking or daydreaming, the Hebrew word implies taking necessary steps to get what we desire.

Covet No One's House

We're not to covet our neighbor's house. It's healthy and holy to want a house, for to make a home, we need a *place* to live. We need a house. Most of us know our family is our most precious earthly society, and a family needs a place in which to live. We need houses—actual physical structures—if we're to make homes, and we need homes in order to live well. Homeless people, dispossessed, rootless, and disrespected, inevitably suffer. There's something simply wrong about being homeless, even when you're homeless by choice.

So we're right when we seek to secure and protect our

homes. As Samuel Johnson said, "To be happy at home is the end of all human endeavour." Those words are worth remembering. The good life stands rooted in the home. Thus, Bret Harte rightly observed that "nobody shoulders a rifle in defense of a boarding house."[1] Few of us would shed our blood to defend a college dormitory or a science lab, though in times of war we will fight to defend our homes. In part, the American Revolution was fought, as James Otis insisted, because "a man's house is his castle; and whilst he is quiet, he is well guarded as a prince in his castle."[2]

Now a house is not automatically a home. But it's difficult to have a home without a house. We're physical creatures, and we need physical structures to live in. So houses, structures made of brick and stone and wood and nails, are important. Like food for the body, houses provide the material elements needed to thrive. We rightly want to build and beautify, to protect and preserve, a house.

My wife and I live in a townhouse in San Diego that adequately meets our needs. Over the years she has papered and painted and redecorated, making the house a home, literally leaving her fingerprints all over it. Her personality is traced in the decor of our home. It's *ours;* we feel we have certain inalienable *rights* to it; and we thank the Lord for it. So it's OK to want a house, and it's good to own a house, the physical shelter enclosing the space we need for a home.

When I walk to school, however, I see the house of one of my friends, perched on a lofty hillside, with a commanding view of San Diego. His house has more space, a nicer view, and is worth far more than mine. I could begin, while walking to school, coveting his house—wanting its space (since I've run out of room for my books), wanting its view (since I like grand vistas), wanting its resale value (since I want financial security). If I did so, I'd break the tenth commandment. To want for myself what my neighbor owns, to will to get what is his, would be to covet.

That's precisely what happened in ancient Israel 700 years before Christ. As the prophet Micah cried, "Woe to those who plan iniquity, to those who plot evil on their beds! At morning's light they carry it out because it is in their power to do it. They covet fields and seize them, and houses, and take them. They defraud a man of his home, a fellowman of his inheritance" (2:1-2).

And that's what's too often happened in America—most visibly as covetous frontiersmen grabbed the land occupied by various American Indian tribes. The year following the 1876 Battle of the Little Bighorn, the Sioux leader Sitting Bull spoke to his people. He noted that "we have now to deal with another race—small and feeble when our fathers first met them but now great and overbearing. Strangely enough, they have a mind to till the soil, and the love of possession is a disease with them."[3] Though not a theologian, not even a Christian, Sitting Bull rightly diagnosed the sin of covetousness, "the love of possession," which was truly a "disease," desiring to get others' houses and lands.

The pioneers' love of possession could be clearly seen by indigenous leaders such as Sitting Bull. Less obvious, but equally pernicious, is the class envy that flourishes in today's welfare state and tramples on private property rights. Zealous advocates of the "social gospel," self-styled prophets of "social justice," easily slip into confiscating private property, which is the very *good* protected by the tenth commandment! They're more than willing to "remove" their "neighbour's landmark" (Deut. 19:14, KJV), just as long as they're taking from the rich to grant entitlements to the poor.

Following socialist dogma, a variety of political leaders have appealed to those who have little, promising to give them money or lands that they seize through legislative or bureaucratic means. With his usual insight, Aristotle wrote in *Politics*, centuries before Christ,

> Such legislation [taking private property] may have a specious appearance of benevolence; men readily listen to it, and are easily induced to believe that in some wonderful manner everybody will become everybody's friend, especially when someone is heard denouncing the evils now existing in states, . . . which are said to arise out of the possession of private property. These evils, however, are due to a very different cause—the wickedness of human nature.[4]

Such perennial realism, part of the common sense philosophical tradition, entered into the substance of the American republic. Thus, the principal architect of the United States Constitution, James Madison, said, "Government is instituted to protect property of every sort as well as individual rights. This being the end of government, that alone is a *just* government that *impartially* secures to every man whatever is his own" (emphases added).

To live under the rule of law, securely controlling one's property, truly liberates a person and helps establish the good life. Real freedom, as Friedrich A. Hayek declared, is "always freedom under the law."[5] In his classic economic work, *The Road to Serfdom*, Hayek wrote: "The Rule of Law . . . implies limits to the scope of legislation," forbidding laws "aimed at particular people or at enabling anybody to use the coercive power of the state" to secure personal or class gains.[6]

Don't Covet Others' Spouses and Servants

Not only must we not covet houses and lands, but also we must not covet the persons who make up our neighbor's household. The text says, "You shall not covet your neighbor's wife" (Exod. 20:17). In part, this means we must not entertain lustful, adulterous desires for our neighbor's husband or wife. Sometimes a woman working in an office may seek to seduce a married man, to involve him in an affair, hoping to shatter his marriage so she can replace his wife. What she wants is not so much sexual pleasure as the economic security and social standing she would enjoy as his wife. Her motivation is covetous. A man might seduce a beautiful woman, breaking up her marriage, in order to marry her and install her as *his* wife, lending her beauty and charm to his household. His inward desire is rightly termed covetous.

Since technology has largely replaced household servants, the literal meaning of part of this commandment cannot be pressed too far. There are, of course, rich folks who employ servants—gardeners, maids. When I ride the San Diego city bus, I'm often surrounded by women who commute from Tijuana, Mexico, to work in wealthy San Diegans' homes. I could envy the wealthy people who can afford servants. My wife might be tempted to covet a full-time maid—though what she would do in our townhouse I'm not sure.

Yet, even if we have no human servants, we are tempted to covet the mechanical "servants" others have. There are tools that make life easier, household appliances that add comfort and validate affluence, machines that literally harness the power of hundreds of horses, which we easily covet. Keeping up with the Joneses exhausts our energies and ingenuity when the Jones family seems forever able to buy the latest gizmo.

Don't Covet Others' Power for Work and Transport

Next, we're told not to covet our neighbor's ox or donkey. In the ancient world, oxen pulled plows—they were the sources of power, the means whereby one prospered. (Oxen, in case you're curious, are cattle bred to do heavy work. Today we breed steers to eat, or milch cows to give milk, but in ancient times people bred cattle to serve as tractors.) To own lots of oxen enabled one to plow lots of land and make lots of money. So it was easy, especially if you had no oxen at all, to covet your neighbor's livestock.

To be honest with you, I've never been tempted to covet an ox. I couldn't care for one if I owned it. But I'm tempted to covet the power sources that enable folks in our society to succeed. I'm tempted to covet the job, the position, the office of those who appear to be more successful than I.

We all need to work. That's just part of being human. And it's fine to try to find the best job, the work that's right for us. It's fine to want to improve ourselves by working hard and getting even better jobs. It's not covetous to want to do well, to succeed, to advance in our vocation. To attain that end, we obviously need tools such as education, skilled ways to do well.

What's wrong is *scheming* to get the position, the office, the authority held by another person. At the college where I work, I have a dual position: professor and chaplain. As a professor, it's fine for me to want to do my best, to move up the promotional track from assistant professor to associate professor to full professor. But if I think my department chairman has more influence and authority than I have, and if I want to get his position, I'd be guilty of covetousness. If I wanted to get the academic dean's position, I'd be coveting. If I wanted to become president of the college and hatched plots to dislodge the present president, I'd be covetous. The Bible simply tells me to be content with what I have, to do my best with what's been given me, to work hard and try to succeed, but not to succeed at others' expense or loss.

Finally, "you shall not covet your neighbor's . . . donkey." Again, I've never seen a donkey I've wanted. You give me a donkey, and I'll try to give it away as soon as possible! But in the ancient world, of course, donkeys were sturdy transportation vehicles. They served as cars and trucks.

So, to contextualize the commandment: "You shall not desire to get your neighbor's automobile." Most clearly, of course, this means we're not to dream up schemes to steal cars. But, short of that, we're not to resent not having what others have. Automobile advertisements, of course, encourage us to feel we're somehow inadequate as human beings if we're not driving a sleek, low-mileage machine.

There's a standard joke on university campuses pointing out the difference between cars parked in faculty parking lots and those in student lots. Professors often drive beat-up old economy models, while students seem able to afford BMWs, Mercedeses, Corvettes, and so on. Sometimes, however, the jokes disguise a certain resentment, a covetousness, which is wrong. We teachers have willingly embraced a profession whose rewards are not primarily monetary. To envy those whose work delivers greater financial dividends—our students' parents and, in time, many of our students themselves—makes us covetous.

I have an old 1972 Chevy pickup, which is all the truck I now need. I need not envy a student who drives a newer truck. I should be glad I have a truck that meets my needs. I have a 1988 Ford that still runs fine and provides my wife and me with reliable transportation. If I've not inflated my ego with the model of my car, I need not worry that my worth as a person may deteriorate along with my aging auto.

Here the words of Theodore Roosevelt ring true: "Probably the greatest harm done by vast wealth is the harm that we of moderate means do to ourselves when we let the vices of envy and hatred enter deep into our own natures."

The central truth of the tenth commandment can be discerned in a story Tolstoy told a century ago. There was a certain Russian peasant who, as most peasants do, wanted more land so as to make a better living for himself and his family. As luck would have it, one day a wealthy landowner offered the peasant a deal to beat all deals—he could have all the land he could walk around in a day.

At the break of dawn on the assigned day, the peasant began walking. He had calculated a reasonable amount of land to encircle, but as he walked, his vision expanded. Thus, as he tried to make it back to the starting point by nightfall, he found himself both tired and needing to exert even more energy to make it. With great difficulty, he strained and strained, jogging as well as walking, and just barely made it back in time. At the moment he finished, however, his heart failed, and he fell dead on the land he had just claimed![7] That's covetousness—wanting more than we need, killing ourselves to possess what we have no right to own.

How truly the old German proverb summed it up: "Charity gives itself rich; covetousness hoards itself poor."

NEW TESTAMENT INTERNALIZATION: SIMPLICITY—WHEN ALL YOU'VE EVER WANTED ISN'T ENOUGH

Many of us, seekers of the "American Dream," easily embrace a radio preacher's corruption of a familiar scripture: "It's not the love of money that's the root of all evil," "Rev. Ike" often declared. "It's the lack of money that's the root of all evil!" "Rev. Ike," perhaps unknowingly, quoted a quip of Mark Twain, and in so doing he echoed a prominent refrain of our culture.

That theme shone through a speech that noted Wall Street financier Ivan Boesky made at the University of California, Berkeley, speaking at the School of Business commencement ceremony. He said, "Greed is good. I want you to know greed is healthy. You can be greedy and feel good about it."[8] At that good news, "the gospel à la Boesky," the budding MBAs and entrepreneurs laughed and applauded.

Boesky's encomium to greed, however, seems strangely ironic in view of his subsequent conviction for stealing $300 million through financial fraud. He was in time brought to trial, found guilty, and imprisoned. I wonder if, after paying $50 million in fines, repaying $50 million to investors, and doing time in prison, Boesky sustained the same enthusiasm for the goodness of greed. I wonder if "you can be greedy and feel good about it" in prison.

Contra Boesky, John the apostle warned against the "lust of the eyes" (1 John 2:16, KJV), the infinite, avaricious desire we men and women have to accumulate possessions, especially money. We're born with a spiritual astigmatism, an *unlimited* capacity for infinite desires. The Old Testament's warning against covetousness, set forth in the tenth commandment, is deepened in the New Testament to a warning against unlimited desires.

Money Draws Us ("People . . . want to get rich")

In Paul's first letter to Timothy we find a passage that follows a warning against those who pervert the way of Jesus into a "success gospel."

"People who want to get rich fall into temptation and a trap and into many foolish and harmful desires that plunge men into ruin and destruction. For the love of money is a root of all kinds of evil. Some people, eager for money, have wandered from the faith and pierced themselves with many griefs" (6:9-10).

Like an enormous electromagnet, money tugs continuously at a tiny bit of shrapnel buried deep within each of our hearts. Its pervasive power indwells popular expressions. "Another day, another dollar"—indicating money gives meaning to the day. "You get what you pay for"—suggesting the worth of goods and services can be reduced to dollars and cents. "The almighty dollar"—indicating it's omnipotent. "Money talks"—most of us agree with Richard Armour, who said, "That money talks I'll not deny; I heard it once—it said good-bye!"[9]

Whereas ancient heroes were admired for their courage and medieval heroes were venerated for their sanctity, modern heroes are vaunted for making money—lots of money! Michael Jordan gets an annual eight-figure income for playing basketball. Michael Jackson signed a multibillion-dollar contract for his musical talents. Heavyweight boxing champions get millions for pounding on their opponents for a few minutes. Even the guys who *get* pounded get millions for their pain!

We easily assume the importance of money, its almost sacred quality, because we live in a world that has routinely been structured by the notion that a man's life, a woman's worth, "consist[s] in the abundance of possessions" (Luke 12:15, NRSV). At times we're tempted to think our consumer society has introduced a totally new issue into the current of our moral life, that never before has money been such a powerful compulsion.

We find, however, when we read the Bible, that it's an ancient issue. Some things rarely change. As sinful men and women, our gods forever remain avarice and greed. Gluttons may want too much food, but they usually reach a limit of consumption—if nothing else, collapsing on the floor when overfilled, or dying of flabby hearts no longer able to endure clogged arteries. There are, after all, limits to how many ice cream sundaes a person can consume. But there's no limit to the amount of money we can deposit in the bank. So money looks infinitely desirable.

Just as the human eye can literally take in the universe (a scientist friend assures me that the eye could actually see all the electrons of the universe if they were large enough!), so the human heart endlessly craves more and more money. John D. Rockefeller was once asked how much money he needed to be content. He answered, "Just a little bit more." Just a bit more—and more—and more. We're drawn to it. We're deceived into thinking a little more money will finally fulfill us, finally make us what we long to be: happy.

Money Damns Us ("A trap . . . ruin and destruction")

That temptation proves fatal our text insists. Wanting to get rich is a temptation, a trap, which leads to ruin and destruction. Rockefeller himself, after getting considerably more than a "little bit more," lamented: "I have made many millions, but they have brought me no happiness. I would barter them all for the days I sat on an office stool in Cleveland and counted myself rich on three dollars a week."[10]

Lots of other millionaires seem to agree. John Jacob Astor, one of the first men to accumulate such a fortune in the pre-Civil War era, said, "I am the most miserable man on earth."[11] Steel magnate Andrew Carnegie lamented, "Millionaires seldom smile."[12] The list could be extended. Admittedly wealth has its comforts. And one must never argue that the poor are automatically more content with life than the rich. But it's clear that money by itself doesn't make folks happy. Those who have most loved and singularly pursued money often testify to its vanity.

What the love of money does to us is separate us from God, displacing Him as the focus of our love. Thus, Raissa Maritain said, "You lack simplicity when you are far from God."[13] Medieval mystic Ruysbroeck said, "Simplicity of intention is the principle and completion of all virtue." That's true, basically, because Jesus said, "Blessed are the pure in heart, for they will see God" (Matt. 5:8). When our vision is clouded by dust clouds of possessions, we fail to see God. When we're rummaging around in the cellars of our own mind, when we're gazing like Narcissus into a pool reflecting our own visage, we'll never see God.

Far from God, we fail to find happiness, for real happiness comes only when we're rightly related to Him. Simplicity sees through the vanity of things with tarnish to treasure the truths of the mind, the beauty of the imagination, the joys of the heart. Money damns us, not because it's intrinsically evil, but because it diverts us from our true vocation in life—loving God.

Simplicity Frees Us ("If we have . . . content")

In Paul's judgment, "Godliness with contentment is great gain. For we brought nothing into the world, and we can take nothing out of it. But if we have food and clothing, we will be content with that" (1 Tim. 6:6-8). To deal with money, many spiritual masters urge us to embrace the second "evangelical counsel," poverty. Since that sounds too radical for many of us, we may, I think, more rightly define it as the contentment that flourishes when we resolve to live simply.

It's obvious that many of us live simply, simply because we have to, not because we want to. But the simplicity that contributes to godliness, the simplicity that contents us, is something deliberately embraced. Simplicity is an inward commitment to live free of money's compulsions, free to follow the will of our Lord. It cultivates what Richard Foster calls the "Freedom of Simplicity."[14]

Simplicity—that's the key to contentment. "Simplicity, simplicity, simplicity!" wrote Henry David Thoreau in *Walden*. "I say, let your affairs be as two or three, and not a hundred or a thousand; instead of a million count half a dozen, and keep your accounts on your thumb-nail."[15]

T. S. Eliot, with his usual precision, calls Christianity "a condition of complete simplicity / (Costing not less than everything)."[16] To that we are called. To live as Christians, we need to live virtuously. If simplicity is a necessary prerequisite for virtue, it follows that we should embrace it. Rather like beginning an exercise program if we want to lose weight, simplifying life is the necessary step to move toward our divinely appointed end, which is the joy that passes understanding.

To simplify our lives is a great art. We need it. Others need it. Planet Earth needs it. Simplicity cleanses our vision to see reality. It helps us see how we ought to live, to see what kinds of persons we ought to be. What we ought to be our text tells us: godly men and women.

So Run! Fight! Hold On!

To live simply, Paul tells us, takes resolve: "But you, man of God, flee from all this, and pursue righteousness, godliness, faith, love, endurance and gentleness. Fight the good fight of the faith. Take hold of the eternal life to which you were called when you made your good confession in the presence of many witnesses" (1 Tim. 6:11-12).

Note the verbs in these verses: flee; pursue; fight; take hold. All denote singularity of purpose, simplicity of action. Like athletes laying aside all that would hinder their performance, like soldiers laying aside their packs in the midst of the battle, believers must simplify their lives in order to be at their best for their Lord.

William James wrote, "Athletes are secular saints, and saints are athletes of God." I'm not a great athlete, but I do enjoy running and run road races when I can. One of the positive things about running is it reduces things to a minimum. You need some good shoes, and that's about it. Golfers may invest thousands of dollars in new equipment and lament the fact that their brand of ball doesn't carry as well as it ought. Tennis players may forever seek to find the perfect racket. But runners simplify things! All you need is a pair of shoes and a willingness to work hard.

And when you race, you don't carry your suitcase. A lot of women beat me in the races I run, but not one of them has ever finished ahead of me carrying her purse. Nor have I ever seen a serious runner with a billfold in his rear pocket. When I line up at the start of a race with a guy who has a Walkman glued to his ears, I know he's no threat—folks may dance to music, but they'll win no races.

So it is in the race of life. To run well, we must lay aside all the stuff that hinders us. And when we do so and run well, there's incredible satisfaction. I can't really explain why aging athletes like me pay good money as entry fees to run races we'll never win. But I do know that when you've trained for a race, and when you run your best, and especially when you establish a personal record, you just feel right with the world.

Indeed: "Athletes are secular saints, and saints are athletes of God." There's no greater joy than fulfilling your potential as a person or as a runner. To do so means we focus singularly on what's good, that we give ourselves without reservation to what's fundamentally joyous. Doing that entails a radical simplicity of intent and action.

Paul summed it up this way:

> Do you not know that in a race all the runners run, but only one gets the prize? Run in such a way as to get the prize. Everyone who competes in the games goes into strict training. They do it to get a crown that will not last; but we do it to get a crown that will last forever. Therefore I do not run like a man running aimlessly; I do not fight like a man beating the air. No, I beat my body and make it my slave so that after I have preached to others, I myself will not be disqualified for the prize (1 Cor. 9:24-27).

Paul's truth recently dawned on one of America's richest men. In response to a "spiritual reawakening" triggered by disillusionment with his vast collection of possessions, Thomas Monaghan, the founder of Domino's Pizza, suddenly began selling off many of his prized possessions, including three houses designed by Frank Lloyd Wright and 30 vintage automobiles, one a $13 million Bugatti. Construction was halted on his new $5 million home, and there was even talk of selling his Detroit Tigers baseball team if he found it to be "a source of excessive pride." He was quoted as saying, "None of the things I've bought, and I mean none of them, have ever really made me happy."[17]

Yet the Lord would like us to be happy—happy in the blessed sense of the Lord Jesus' beatitudes. Jesus Christ began that list of "blessed" characteristics with the words "Blessed are the poor in spirit" (Matt. 5:3). That, in part, is the spirit that eschews covetousness, the person who is happy to say, "Enough's enough."

Notes

Chapter 1

1. Quoted in William Murchison, *Reclaiming Morality in America* (Nashville: Thomas Nelson, 1994), 1.

2. Ibid., 55.

3. Ibid., 86.

4. Tim and Beverly LaHaye, *A Nation Without a Conscience* (Wheaton, Ill.: Tyndale House, 1994), 19.

5. James Patterson and Peter Kim, *The Day America Told the Truth: What People Really Believe About Everything That Really Matters* (New York: Prentice Hall Press, 1991), 41.

6. Allan Bloom, *The Closing of the American Mind* (New York: Simon and Schuster, 1987), 19.

7. Ibid., 21.

8. Ernest Hemingway, *Death in the Afternoon* (New York: Scribners, 1932), 4.

9. Bloom, *Closing of the American Mind*, 141.

10. *First Things* 45 (August-September 1994): 20-21.

11. Quoted in William Murchison, *Reclaiming Morality in America*, 53.

12. Manis Friedman, *Doesn't Anyone Blush Anymore? Reclaiming Intimacy, Modesty, and Sexuality in a Permissive Age* (San Francisco: Harper, 1990).

13. Daniel Smith-Rowsey, "The Terrible Twenties," *Newsweek*, June 17, 1991, unnumbered page.

14. Quoted in Robert H. Schuller, *Believe in the God Who Believes in You* (New York: Bantam Books, 1991), 93-94.

15. John Paul II, *The Splendor of Truth—Veritatus Splendor* (Boston: St. Paul Books and Media, 1993), 104.

16. Ibid., 125.

Chapter 2

1. W. H. Auden, "September 1, 1939," in *Collected Poetry of W. H. Auden* (New York: Random House, 1945), 58.

2. Augustine, *Divine Providence and the Problem of Evil*, trans. Robert P. Russell, vol. 5 of *Writings of St. Augustine, Fathers of the Church* (New York: CIMA Publishing Co., 1948), 279.

3. Elizabeth Barrett Browning, *Aurora Leigh* (New York: Worthington Co., 1890), book vii.

4. *The International Thesaurus of Quotations*, comp. Rhoda T. Tripp (New York: Thomas V. Crowell, Publisher, 1970), 986.

5. "Living by Vows," *Christianity Today*, October 8, 1990, 38-40.

6. T. S. Eliot, "Choruses from 'The Rock,'" in *The Complete Poems and Plays* (New York: Harcourt, Brace and World, 1962), 103.

7. These phrases resonate with lines in T. S. Eliot's "The Love Song of J. Alfred Prufrock," ibid., 4-7.

8. "Life in These United States," *Reader's Digest,* October 1987, 170.

9. The author made a considerable effort to locate the source for this and other undocumented quotations and illustrations. Appropriate credit, if known, will be included in any reprinting.

Chapter 3

1. Philip Johnson, *Darwin on Trial* (Downers Grove, Ill.: InterVarsity Press, 1991).

2. Ibid., 13.

3. Ibid., 14.

4. Ibid.

5. Quoted ibid., 9.

6. Ibid., 128.

7. Ibid., 114.

8. Ibid., 130.

9. Quoted in Scott M. Huse, *The Collapse of Evolution,* 2nd ed. (Grand Rapids: Baker Book House, 1993), 3.

10. Patterson and Kim, *Day America Told the Truth,* 73.

11. Ibid., 72.

12. *Degenerate Moderns: Modernity as Rationalized Sexual Misbehavior* by Michael E. Jones. © 1993 Ignatius Press, San Francisco. All rights reserved; reprinted with permission of Ignatius Press.

13. Ibid., 11.

14. Ibid., 12.

15. Ibid., 17.

16. Ibid., 39.

17. Ibid., 181.

18. George Moriarty, "The Road Ahead of the Road Behind," quoted in John Wooden, *They Call Me Coach* (Waco, Tex.: Word Books, 1973), 1.

19. *The Little Brown Book of Anecdotes,* ed. Clifton Fadiman (Boston: Little, Brown and Co., 1985), 15.

20. C. S. Lewis, *Surprised by Joy* (New York: Harcourt Brace, 1955), 228.

21. *International Thesaurus of Quotations,* 965.

22. Quoted in *Whatever It Is, I'm Against It,* comp. and ed. Nat Shapiro (New York: Simon and Shuster, 1984), 265-66.

23. Neil Postman, *Amusing Ourselves to Death* (New York: Penguin Books, 1985).

24. Ibid., 8.

25. Ibid., 63.

26. *Little Brown Book of Anecdotes,* 439. Paige had a business card he gave young fans with "Six Rules for a Happy Life." Rule number 6 was "Don't look back. Something may be gaining on you."

Chapter 4

1. Annie Dillard, "Tickets for a Prayer Wheel," in *Tickets for a Prayer Wheel* (New York: Harper and Row, 1974), 125-27.

2. *The Encyclopedia of Religious Quotations,* comp. and ed. Frank S. Mead (Westwood, N.J.: Fleming H. Revell, 1965), 243.

3. "Casual Observations," *Mr. Dooley's Philosophy* (1900), quoted in *International Thesaurus of Quotations,* 333. Dunne used Mr. Dooley as a pen name.

4. Quoted in Julian Huxley, *Perennial Philosophy* (New York: Harper and Row, 1970), 252.

5. Joy Davidman, *Smoke on the Mountain: An Interpretation of the Ten Commandments* (Philadelphia: Westminster Press, 1954), 39.

6. Ernesto Cardinal, *To Live Is to Love* (New York: Herder and Herder, 1972), 101.

7. Tony Campolo, *The Success Fantasy* (Wheaton, Ill.: Victor Books, 1980), 12.

8. L. S. Stavrianos, *The Promise of the Coming Dark Ages* (San Francisco: W. H. Freeman, 1976), 40.

9. William Barclay, *The Gospel of Matthew* (Philadelphia: Westminster Press, 1956), 1:244.

10. Frederick Dale Bruner, *The Christbook* (Waco, Tex.: Word Books, 1987), 264.

11. Ibid.

12. Ibid.

13. Quoted in W. H. Auden, *A Certain World* (New York: Viking Press, 1970), 266.

14. Jacques Ellul, *Money and Power* (Downers Grove, Ill.: InterVarsity Press, 1984), 75.

15. E. F. Schumacher, *Small Is Beautiful* (New York: Harper and Row, 1973), 24.

16. Ibid.

17. Patterson and Kim, *Day America Told the Truth,* 65-66.

18. *McCall's,* September 1990, 57.

19. Ellul, *Money and Power,* 76.

20. John Kenneth Galbraith, *Money* (Boston: Houghton Mifflin, 1975), 4.

21. *Encyclopedia of 7,700 Illustrations,* comp. Paul Lee Tan (Rockville, Md.: Assurance Publishers, 1984), 288-89.

22. Barclay's view.

23. William Barclay, *The Gospel of Matthew,* 2nd ed. (Philadelphia: Westminster Press, 1958), 1:244.

Chapter 5

1. Quoted in R. H. Charles, *The Decalogue* (Edinburgh: T. and T. Clark, 1923), 89.

2. *Time,* May 7, 1990, cover.

3. Mark Twain, *Notebook* (1935), in *International Thesaurus of Quotations,* 625.

4. Davidman, *Smoke on the Mountain,* 42-43.

5. David A. Seamands, *God's Blueprint for Living: New Perspectives on the Ten Commandments* (Wilmore, Ky.: Bristol Books, 1988), 52.

6. Davidman, *Smoke on the Mountain*, 43.

7. Randal Earl Denny, *Tables of Stone for Modern Living* (Kansas City: Beacon Hill Press of Kansas City, 1970), 31.

8. Davidman, *Smoke on the Mountain*, 46.

9. *Leadership*, summer 1991, 110-14.

10. *Little Brown Book of Anecdotes*, 555.

11. William Lambdin, *Doublespeak Dictionary* (Los Angeles: Pinnacle Books, 1979), 98.

12. Bruner, *Christbook*, 202.

13. Cited in *International Thesaurus of Quotations*, 437.

14. *Little Brown Book of Anecdotes*, 55. The newspaper *Frana-Sois* reported the incident, allegedly provided by an eyewitness who was a member of the presidium.

15. Chief Joseph, quoted in *I Have Spoken: American History Through the Voices of the Indians*, comp. Virginia Irving Armstrong (New York: Pocket Books, 1972), 134.

16. Bruner, *Christbook*, 291.

17. C. S. Lewis, *Letters to Malcolm: Chiefly on Prayer* (New York: Harcourt Brace Jovanovich, 1964), 75.

18. Quoted in *Herald of Holiness*, August 19, 1970, 11.

Chapter 6

1. *International Thesaurus of Quotations*, 276.

2. Abraham Joshua Heschel, *The Sabbath: Its Meaning for Modern Man* (New York: Farrar, Straus and Giroux, 1951), 3-4.

3. Jürgen Moltmann, *God in Creation* (San Francisco: Harper and Row, 1985), 280.

4. C. S. Lewis, "Historicism," in *Christian Reflections* (Grand Rapids: William B. Eerdmans, 1967), 113.

5. Will Rogers, *The Autobiography of Will Rogers* (New York: Rogers Publishing, 1949), 15.

6. James Houston, *I Believe in the Creator* (Grand Rapids: William B. Eerdmans, 1980), 162.

7. Paul W. Brand, "'A Handful of Mud': A Personal History of My Love for the Soil," in *Tending the Garden: Essays on the Gospel and the Earth*, ed. Wesley Granberg-Michaelson (Grand Rapids: William B. Eerdmans, 1987), 147.

8. From *To the Magnesians*, 9.

9. Quoted in Charles, *Decalogue*, 139.

10. Augustine, *Confessions*, 10.22.

Chapter 7

1. Quoted in Michael J. Gorman, *Abortion and the Early Church: Christian, Jewish, and Pagan Attitudes in the Greco-Roman World* (Downers Grove, Ill.: InterVarsity Press, 1982), 28.

2. Bryce J. Christensen, *Utopia Against the Family: The Problems and Politics of the American Family* (San Francisco: Ignatius Press, 1990). Christensen edits *The Family in America* and directs the Rockford Center Institute on the Family.

3. T. S. Eliot, "Choruses from 'The Rock,'" 106.

4. Christensen, *Utopia Against the Family*, 36.

5. Ibid., 40.

6. Ibid., 68.

7. Sara McLanahan and Gary Sandefur, *Growing Up with a Single Parent: What Hurts, What Helps* (Cambridge: Harvard University Press, 1994), 1.

8. Dr. Dobson told this story when he spoke at MidAmerica Nazarene College in Olathe, Kansas, when I was on the faculty in the 1970s.

9. Napoléon Bonaparte, *Maxims* (1804-15), quoted in *International Thesaurus of Quotations*, 141.

10. Dietrich Bonhoeffer, *A Testament of Freedom* (New York: Harper-Collins, 1990), 53.

11. Ibid., 109.

12. Ibid., 537.

13. Cited in *International Thesaurus of Quotations*, 248.

14. Bruner, *Christbook*, 393.

15. Sidney Ahlstrom, *A Religious History of the American People* (New Haven, Conn.: Yale University Press, 1932), 864-65.

Chapter 8

1. This story appeared in an issue of Chuck Colson's *Prison Fellowship Newsletter* (date unavailable).

2. Francis J. Beckwith, *Politically Correct Death: Answering Arguments for Abortion Rights* (Grand Rapids: Baker Book House, 1993).

3. Ibid., 34.

4. Ibid., 41.

5. Ibid., 42.

6. Ibid., 43.

7. Ibid., 53.

8. See Gorman, *Abortion and the Early Church*, 54.

9. Ibid., 29.

10. Ibid., 28.

11. Ibid., 54.

12. Bruner, *Christbook*, 175.

13. *Little Brown Book of Anecdotes*, 422.

14. Ibid., 298.

15. Ibid., 32.

16. Ibid., 47.

Chapter 9

1. *Time*, June 23, 1967, n.p.

2. Patterson and Kim, *Day America Told the Truth*, 94-99.

3. Ibid., 96.

4. *Little Brown Book of Anecdotes*, 227.

5. Andrew Greeley, *Faithful Attraction: Discovering Intimacy, Love, and Fidelity in American Marriage* (New York: Tom Doherty Associates, 1991).

6. Ibid., 20.

7. Ibid., 22-24.

8. Ibid., 221.

9. Ibid., 55.

10. Ibid., 63.

11. Ibid., 69.

12. Ibid., 229.

13. Ibid., 230.

14. Albert Camus, *The Fall* (1957), quoted in Robert Byrne, *1,911 Best Things Anybody Ever Said* (New York: Fawcett Columbine, 1988), 113.

15. Friedman, *Doesn't Anyone Blush Anymore?* 64.

16. Mark Twain, "Pudd'nhead Wilson's New Calendar," in *Following the Equator*, in *The Portable Mark Twain* (New York: Viking Press, 1946), 564.

17. Quotation from Ingmar Bergman, *The Magic Lantern: An Autobiography* (New York: Viking, 1988), in a book review in *Time*, September 26, 1988, 104.

18. A December 1991 article in *McCall's* stresses that personal intimacy is one of the "five dimensions" of healthy marriages, far more important than sexual performance.

19. Josh McDowell, *Why Wait?* (Waco, Tex.: Word Publishing, 1994), 125.

20. Friedman, *Doesn't Anyone Blush Anymore?* 64.

Chapter 10

1. Davidman, *Smoke on the Mountain*, 97.

2. Ibid., 97-98.

3. John Killinger, *To My People with Love: The Ten Commandments for Today* (Nashville: Abingdon Press, 1988), 91-92.

4. Theodore Pappas, "Plagiarism, Culture, and the Future of the Academy," in *The Martin Luther King, Jr., Plagiarism Story*, ed. Theodore Pappas (Rockford, Ill.: Rockford Institute, 1994), 26.

5. These are listed on p. 66 of the August 20, 1992, issue.

6. *Illustrations for Biblical Preaching*, ed. Michael P. Green (Grand Rapids: Baker Book House, 1989), 194.

7. *Little Brown Book of Anecdotes*, 327.

8. Lawrence J. Peter, *Peter's Quotations* (New York: Bantam Books, 1979), 535.

9. Ibid.

10. Fyodor Dostoyevsky, *A Diary of a Writer* (1873), quoted in *International Thesaurus of Quotations*, 107.

11. Eric Gill, *A Holy Tradition of Working: An Anthology of the Writing of Eric Gill* (West Stockbridge, Mass.: Lindisfarne Press, 1983), 58.

12. Marvella McDill, contributor to "All in a Day's Work," *Reader's Digest*, October 1988, 121.

13. "Immortal Remark," *New York Herald Tribune*, September 29, 1954, in George Seldes, *The Great Quotations* (New York: Pocket Books, 1967), 986.

14. Peter, *Peter's Quotations*, 536.

15. Ibid., 537.

16. Chuck Colson and Jack Eckerd, *Why America Doesn't Work* (Dallas: Word Publishing, 1991), 110.

17. David Ben-Gurion, statement given March 19, 1946, to the Anglo-American Commission of Inquiry, quoted in Seldes, *Great Quotations*, 985.

18. Gill, *Holy Tradition of Working*, 125.

19. Harry Emerson Fosdick, *The Meaning of Prayer* (New York: Abingdon Press, 1915), 64.

Chapter 11

1. Chuck Colson, *A Dance with Deception* (Dallas: Word Publishing, 1993), 70.

2. *Little Brown Book of Anecdotes*, 513.

3. Robert I. Kahn, *The Letter and the Spirit* (Waco, Tex.: Word Books, 1972), 70.

4. Adolf Hitler, *Mein Kampf* (1924) 1.10, quoted in *International Thesaurus of Quotations*, 205.

5. From *The Public Papers and Addresses of Franklin D. Roosevelt*, 8:517 (October 30, 1940), quoted in Sissela Bok, *Lying: Moral Choice in Public and Private Life* (New York: Vintage Books, 1978), 189.

6. Quoted in Theodore White, *The Making of a President 1964* (New York: Atheneum, 1965), 373.

7. David Broder, "Clinton Shouldn't Overlook That Fourth Deficit: Trust," *San Diego Union*, February 25, 1993.

8. Quoted in James Thomas Flexner, *George Washington: The Forge of Experience* (Boston: Little, Brown and Co., 1965), 257.

9. Bok, *Lying*, 19.

10. Benito Mussolini, "Instructions to Fernando Mezzasoma," in Seldes, *Great Quotations*, 607.

11. Friedrich Nietzsche, *The Will to Power*, quoted in Bok, *Lying*, 18.

12. Bill Walsh, "The Case for Kudos," *Forbes ASAP*, October 1994, 17.

13. Ibid.

14. Ibid.

15. C. S. Lewis, *Reflections on the Psalms* (San Diego: Harcourt Brace Jovanovich, 1958), 94.

16. Ibid.

17. Gary Smalley and John Trent, *The Blessing* (Nashville: Thomas Nelson, 1986).

18. Ibid., 47-48.

19. Ben Jonson, *Timber; On Discoveries* (1640).

Chapter 12

1. Peter, *Peter's Quotations*, 245.

2. James Otis, speech against the writs of assistance, February 24, 1761, quoted in *International Thesaurus of Quotations*, 283.

3. T. C. McLuhan, *Touch the Earth* (New York: Pocket Books, 1972), 90.

4. Aristotle, *Politics* 2.5, trans. Benjamin Jowett.

5. Gottfried Dietze, "Hayek on the Rule of Law," in *Essays on Hayek*, ed. Fritz Machlup (Hillsdale, Mich.: Hillsdale College Press, 1976), 110.

6. Friedrich A. Hayek, *The Road to Serfdom* (Chicago: Phoenix Books, 1944), 83-84.

7. Denny, *Tables of Stone for Modern Living*, 111.

8. Quoted by Richard Halverson (chaplain of the United States Senate), address given at Conference on Biblical Exposition, Anaheim, Calif., 1985.

9. Peter, *Peter's Quotations*, 346.

10. *Encyclopedia of 7,700 Illustrations*, 827.

11. Ibid.

12. Ibid.

13. Raissa Maritain, *We Have Been Friends Together* (Garden City, N.Y.: Image Books, 1961), 136.

14. Title of a book written by Foster.

15. Henry David Thoreau, "Where I Live, and What I Lived For," in *Walden* (1854), quoted in *International Thesaurus of Quotations*, 592.

16. Eliot, "Little Gidding," in *Complete Poems and Plays*, 145.

17. Thomas H. Naylor, "The Living Dead," *New Oxford Review* 59, No. 4 (September 1992): 26.

Resources for Further Reading

Barclay, William. *The Old Law and the New Law*. Philadelphia: Westminster Press, 1972.

———. *The Ten Commandments for Today*. San Francisco: Harper San Francisco, 1973.

Bonhoeffer, Dietrich. *The Cost of Discipleship*. Rev. ed. New York: Macmillan Co., 1963.

Brooks, Roger. *The Spirit of the Ten Commandments: Shattering the Myth of Rabbinic Legalism*. San Francisco: Harper and Row, 1990.

Chappell, Clovis. *Ten Rules for Living*. Nashville: Abingdon, 1966.

Charles, R. H. *The Decalogue*. Edinburgh: T. and T. Clark, 1923.

Davidman, Joy. *Smoke on the Mountain: An Interpretation of the Ten Commandments*. Philadelphia: Westminster Press, 1954.

Denny, Randal Earl. *Tables of Stone for Modern Living*. Kansas City: Beacon Hill Press of Kansas City, 1970.

Harrelson, Walter J. *The Ten Commandments and Human Rights*. Philadelphia: Fortress Press, 1980.

Heschel, Abraham Joshua. *God in Search of Man: A Philosophy of Judaism*. New York: Farrar, Strauss, and Giroux, 1955.

———. *The Sabbath: Its Meaning for Modern Man*. New York: Farrar, Strauss, and Giroux, 1951.

Kahn, Robert I. *The Letter and the Spirit*. Waco, Tex.: Word Books, 1972.

Killinger, John. *To My People with Love: The Ten Commandments for Today*. Nashville: Abingdon Press, 1988.

Lewis, C. S. *The Abolition of Man*. New York: Macmillan Co., 1947.

———. *Christian Reflections*. Grand Rapids: William B. Eerdmans, 1967.

———. *Mere Christianity*. New York: Macmillan Co., 1952.

Schuller, Robert H. *Believe in the God Who Believes in You*. New York: Bantam Books, 1991.

Seamands, David A. *God's Blueprint for Living: New Perspectives on the Ten Commandments*. Wilmore, Ky.: Bristol Books, 1988.

Smedes, Lewis B. *Mere Morality: What God Expects from Ordinary People*. Grand Rapids: William B. Eerdmans, 1983.

Trueblood, Elton. *Foundations for Reconstruction*. New York: Harper and Brothers, 1946.

Williams, Jay G. *Ten Words of Freedom*. Philadelphia: Fortress Press, 1971.